MOVIE ★ ICONS

CONNERY

EDITOR
PAUL DUNCAN

TEXT
ALAIN SILVER

PHOTOS
THE KOBAL COLLECTION

TASCHEN

HONG KONG KÖLN LONDON LOS ANGELES MADRID PARIS TOKYO

CONTENTS

8

SEAN CONNERY: GENUINE
14 SEAN CONNERY: DER ECHTE
18 SEAN CONNERY : L'AUTHENTIQUE
by Alain Silver

22

VISUAL FILMOGRAPHY
22 FILMOGRAFIE IN BILDERN
22 FILMOGRAPHIE EN IMAGES

178

CHRONOLOGY
182 CHRONOLOGIE
184 CHRONOLOGIE

186

FILMOGRAPHY
186 FILMOGRAFIE
186 FILMOGRAPHIE

192

BIBLIOGRAPHY
192 BIBLIOGRAFIE
192 BIBLIOGRAPHIE

1

SEAN CONNERY: GENUINE

BY ALAIN SILVER

SEAN CONNERY: DER ECHTE

SEAN CONNERY: L'AUTHENTIQUE

SEAN CONNERY: GENUINE

by Alain Silver

Sean Connery's official online biography opens with a quote from Steven Spielberg, who asserted—based on their association on *Indiana Jones and the Last Crusade* in 1989, the same year the then 59-year-old Connery was proclaimed the "sexiest man alive"—that "there are seven genuine movie stars in the world today, and Sean is one of them." With this remark often cited by Connery biographers in support of his iconic status, the obvious question is, who are the other six?

Certainly there are stars who have been paid more per picture, stars with bigger fan clubs, more tabloid ink, more awards, more adulation, more cars, more mansions, more of just about anything. One could also characterize some stars as narcissistic, false-hearted, or avaricious. Given his beginnings in a cold-water Edinburgh flat, one could have expected stardom to go to Thomas Sean Connery's head. Instead his youthful experience grounded him in everyday reality. Always a competitor in sports and in life, Connery's outlook was never about winning at any cost. "I never trashed a hotel room. I understand if you get caught in a fight, but to take it out on a room, that implies some psychiatric disorder. The way I was brought up made me think about the person who has to clean up afterwards."

From Mary Pickford on, movie stars have been an American invention. Whatever their origin, "genuine movie stars" have invariably been defined by Hollywood films and the American industry that sustains them. Of the 36 recipients of the American Film Institute Life Achievement Award, 23 have been actors (ten have been directors, and three did some of both acting and directing). Only one of those actors was not American. Why is a Scotsman, then, the only non-American on the AFI's prestigious list? Perhaps it is because Connery's international career made him a "genuine movie star" without any

ON THE SET OF 'GOLDFINGER' (1964)
A signature look in his signature role: sidelight emphasizes chiseled features and penetrating eyes. / Unverwechselbar in der Rolle, die ihn zum Star machte: Die Ausleuchtung von der Seite hebt die kantigen Gesichtszüge und die eindringlichen Augen hervor. / La lumière latérale souligne des traits ciselés et un regard pénétrant : la griffe du rôle qu'il marqua d'une empreinte indélébile.

"I'm an actor. It's not brain surgery. If I do my job right, people won't ask for their money back."
Sean Connery

petty disputation, pretension, or pandering to current fashion. Although he is always ready to speak his mind, often with unexpected bluntness—as he said in announcing his retirement, "I'm fed up with the idiots, the ever-widening gap between people who know how to make movies and those who green-light them"—Connery's fellow filmmakers invariably cite not just his candor but his altruism and humility.

Of his own story, Connery mockingly believes that "it reads as though one had made great dramatic decisions, but in fact one didn't. I certainly had the drive from the beginning ... but the ambitions were much, much less." Like most performers who have risen to worldwide acclaim, Connery must acknowledge his underlying drive to succeed. Unlike many of them, he offers no sham of predestined fame, no assertion that talent would out, simply the belief that "perhaps I'm not a good actor, but I would be even worse at doing anything else."

Like many intuitive actors, writers, and directors, Connery is reluctant to claim any artfulness. Yet Connery admits that, as a bit player in touring companies in the 1950s, he spent much of his spare time in local libraries reading classic plays. Soon thereafter, there was Bond, James Bond. What Connery did with that opportunity is well known. Did Bond make him a "genuine movie star"? Indisputably. Did Connery's incarnation of Bond lay the foundation for the most successful franchise in motion-picture history? Definitely. Together Bond and Connery became larger-than-life; but it was Connery, not Bond, whose powerful presence went on to permeate scores of other roles. "Time moves on, styles move on," noted director Terry Gilliam. "Sean doesn't change: He plays any part and he's always Scottish." Connery can be as cool and charismatic as Steve McQueen, as elegant as Katharine Hepburn, or as generous as Frank Sinatra. What he cannot be is English, because that would be false. His tattoo reads "Scotland Forever," and Connery got his knighthood despite his fervent Scottish nationalism.

Connery has the underlying truth that makes him "genuine" in the estimation of Spielberg and countless others with whom he has worked. Are there another six like that? Not according to another Hepburn, his one-time costar Audrey, who guilelessly affirmed: "There are only two great stars in my recollection who have not been changed by great massive success: Sean Connery and Lassie."

FRONT ENDPAPERS/VORSATZBLÄTTER/
PAGES DE GARDE EN DÉBUT D'OUVRAGE
ARTWORK FOR 'THUNDERBALL' (1965)

BACK ENDPAPERS/NACHSATZBLÄTTER/
PAGES DE GARDE EN FIN D'OUVRAGE
**ARTWORK FOR
'YOU ONLY LIVE TWICE' (1967)**

PAGES 2/3
STILL FROM 'THUNDERBALL' (1965)

PAGE 4
**PORTRAIT FOR
'FROM RUSSIA WITH LOVE' (1963)**

PAGES 6/7
**STILL FROM 'THE LEAGUE OF
EXTRAORDINARY GENTLEMEN' (2003)**

PAGE 8
**PORTRAIT FOR
'DIAMONDS ARE FOREVER' (1971)**

OPPOSITE/RECHTS/PAGE CI-CONTRE
STILL FROM 'OUTLAND' (1981)

SEAN CONNERY: DER ECHTE

von Alain Silver

Sean Connerys offizielle Onlinebiografie beginnt mit einem Zitat von Steven Spielberg, der – auf der Grundlage ihrer Zusammenarbeit in *Indiana Jones und der letzte Kreuzzug* im Jahre 1989, dem gleichen Jahr, in dem der 59-jährige Connery auch zum „sexiest man alive" ernannt wurde – erklärte, es gebe „sieben echte Filmstars in der heutigen Welt, und Sean ist einer von ihnen". Die Frage, die sich aus dieser oft zitierten Feststellung, mit der Connery-Biografen gerne seinen Status als Ikone belegen, ergibt, ist: Wer sind die anderen sechs?

Es gibt sicherlich Stars, die pro Film höhere Gagen einstreichen, Stars mit größeren Fanclubs, mehr Klatschberichten in der Boulevardpresse, mehr Auszeichnungen, mehr Starkult, mehr Autos, mehr Villen, mehr von nahezu allem. Man könnte manche Stars auch als narzisstisch, falsch oder geldgierig charakterisieren. Wenn man bedenkt, dass Connery in einer Wohnung in Edinburgh aufwuchs, in der es nicht einmal warmes Wasser gab, dann wäre es durchaus verständlich gewesen, wenn Thomas Sean Connery der Starruhm zu Kopfe gestiegen wäre. Stattdessen aber verwurzelte ihn seine Jugenderfahrung fest in der Wirklichkeit des Alltags. Er war im Sport wie im Leben stets ein ehrgeiziger Wettkämpfer, aber der Sieg um jeden Preis lag ihm fern. „Ich habe nie ein Hotelzimmer verwüstet. Ich kann verstehen, wenn man in Handgreiflichkeiten verwickelt wird, aber es an einem Zimmer auszulassen, das zeugt doch schon von Geistesstörung. Durch meine Erziehung musste ich an denjenigen denken, der das hinterher aufräumen muss."

Angefangen mit Mary Pickford, waren Filmstars eine amerikanische Erfindung. Unabhängig von ihrer Herkunft wurden „echte Filmstars" unweigerlich von Hollywoodfilmen und der amerikanischen Industrie, auf die sie sich stützen, definiert. Von den 36 Empfängern des „Life Achievement Award" des American Film Institute für ihr Lebenswerk waren 23 Schauspieler (zehn waren Regisseure, und drei waren sowohl Schauspieler als auch Regisseure). Nur einer von ihnen war kein Amerikaner. Warum wurde also ein Schotte der einzige

PORTRAIT FOR 'DARBY O'GILL AND THE LITTLE PEOPLE' (1959)
Walt Disney gives Connery the full star treatment for his first Hollywood film. / In Connerys erstem Hollywoodfilm behandelte Walt Disney ihn schon wie einen Star. / Walt Disney traita Connery comme une vedette à part entière pour son premier film hollywoodien.

„Ich bin Schauspieler. Das ist keine Gehirnchirurgie. Wenn ich meine Sache ordentlich mache, dann werden die Leute schon nicht ihr Geld zurückverlangen."
Sean Connery

Nichtamerikaner auf der prestigeträchtigen Liste des AFI? Vielleicht deshalb, weil Connerys internationale Karriere ihn zu einem „echten Filmstar" machte – ohne kleinliches Gezänk, ohne Allüren und ohne Anpassung an flüchtige Modetrends. Obwohl er nie zögert, seine Meinung kundzutun, und das häufig verblüffend unverblümt – wie beispielsweise, als er seinen Ruhestand mit den Worten ankündigte: „Ich hab die Schnauze voll von diesen Idioten, von der immer größer werdenden Kluft zwischen den Leuten, die wissen, wie man Filme macht, und denen, die ihnen grünes Licht geben" –, wissen Connerys Filmkollegen nicht nur seine Offenheit zu schätzen, sondern auch seine Selbstlosigkeit und seine Bescheidenheit.

Von seiner eigenen Geschichte meint Connery scherzhaft, sie lese „sich so, als habe jemand große dramatische Entscheidungen getroffen, aber in Wirklichkeit war dem nicht so. Ich besaß gewiss von Anfang an den Antrieb ... aber die Ziele und Ambitionen waren sehr viel geringer." Wie die meisten Schauspieler, die es zu Weltruhm gebracht haben, muss Connery den zugrunde liegenden Willen zum Erfolg einräumen. Im Unterschied zu vielen anderen gibt er aber nicht vor, der Ruhm sei ihm in die Wiege gelegt worden oder dass sich Talent zwangsläufig durchsetze, sondern meint lediglich: „Vielleicht bin ich kein guter Schauspieler, aber ich wäre in einem anderen Beruf noch schlechter."

Wie viele Schauspieler, Schriftsteller und Regisseure, die ihrer inneren Stimme folgen, redet Connery nur ungern von Kunstfertigkeit, doch er gibt zu, dass er, als er mit Wanderbühnen in den 1950er-Jahren durch die Lande tingelte und Kleinstrollen spielte, einen großen Teil seiner Freizeit in den örtlichen Bibliotheken verbrachte und Theaterklassiker las. Wenig später war er Bond, James Bond. Was Connery aus dieser Chance machte, ist hinlänglich bekannt. Machte Bond einen „echten Filmstar" aus ihm? Unbestreitbar. Legte Connerys Bond-Darstellung den Grundstein für die erfolgreichste Reihe der Filmgeschichte? Sicherlich. Gemeinsam wuchsen Bond und Connery über das Leben hinaus – doch es war Connery, nicht Bond, dessen mächtige Präsenz Dutzende anderer Rollen prägte. „Die Zeit schreitet fort, die Geschmäcker ändern sich", meinte Regisseur Terry Gilliam. „Sean ändert sich nicht: Er spielt jede Rolle, und er ist stets Schotte." Connery kann so cool und charismatisch sein wie Steve McQueen, so elegant wie Katharine Hepburn oder so großzügig wie Frank Sinatra. Was er nicht sein kann, ist englisch, weil das falsch wäre. Er trägt eine Tätowierung mit den Worten „Scotland Forever" („Schottland auf ewig") und wurde trotz seines glühenden schottischen Nationaleifers zum Ritter geschlagen.

Darum also besitzt Sir Sean Connery jene grundlegende Wahrhaftigkeit, die ihn in den Augen Spielbergs und zahlreicher anderer, mit denen er zusammenarbeitete, „echt" erscheinen lässt. Gibt es noch sechs andere wie ihn? Nicht, wenn man seiner einstigen Schauspielkollegin Audrey Hepburn glaubt, die arglos beteuerte: „In meiner Erinnerung gibt es nur zwei große Stars, die von gewaltigem Erfolg nicht verändert wurden: Sean Connery und Lassie."

PORTRAIT FOR 'A FINE MADNESS' (1966)
Connery always looked for scripts that had an edge or a literary quality about them. / Connery hielt immer Ausschau nach Drehbüchern mit Ecken und Kanten oder mit gewissen literarischen Zügen. / Connery était toujours en quête de scénarios travaillés, littéraires.

SEAN CONNERY : L'AUTHENTIQUE

Alain Silver

La biographie officielle de Sean Connery publiée en ligne s'ouvre sur une citation de Steven Spielberg – avec lequel il tourna *Indiana Jones et la dernière croisade* en 1989, l'année où Connery, à l'âge de 59 ans, fut proclamé l'« homme le plus sexy du monde » : « Il existe sept authentiques stars du cinéma dans le monde aujourd'hui, et Sean en fait partie. » Cette remarque, fréquemment citée par les biographes de Connery pour décrire son caractère emblématique, suscite inévitablement la curiosité quant à l'identité des six autres !

Certes, il existe des stars du cinéma mieux payées, ou entourées de fan-clubs plus importants, et certaines font couler davantage d'encre dans la presse à scandale, sont plus adulées ou possèdent davantage de voitures et de villas de rêve. D'autres pourraient être qualifiées de narcissiques, fourbes ou avares. Thomas Sean Connery ayant grandi dans un appartement sans eau chaude d'Édimbourg, on aurait pu penser que la célébrité lui serait montée à la tête. Mais ses jeunes années difficiles l'ont au contraire ancré dans la réalité quotidienne. Toujours friand de compétition – dans le sport comme dans la vie –, il n'a cependant jamais cherché à gagner à tout prix. « Je n'ai jamais vandalisé une chambre d'hôtel. Je peux comprendre qu'on se trouve embarqué dans une bagarre, mais se défouler sur une chambre, cela relève véritablement d'un déséquilibre psychiatrique. La manière dont j'ai été élevé fait que je pense à la personne qui nettoiera tout après. »

Depuis Mary Pickford, les vedettes du 7ᵉ art sont une invention américaine. Quelle que soit leur origine, les « authentiques stars de cinéma » se sont toujours construites grâce à des films hollywoodiens et à l'industrie américaine qui les alimente. Parmi les 36 lauréats du Life Achievement Award décerné par l'American Film Institute (prix couronnant l'ensemble d'une carrière), 23 sont des acteurs, dix sont des réalisateurs et les trois derniers cumulent les deux casquettes. Un seul de ces comédiens récompensés n'était pas américain. Pourquoi notre Écossais est-il le seul non-Américain à figurer au palmarès de l'American Film Institute ? Peut-être parce que la carrière internationale de Sean Connery a fait de lui une « authentique star du cinéma » sans qu'il cède jamais aux querelles mesquines, à la prétention ou aux

STILL FROM 'THE NAME OF THE ROSE' (1986)
Brother William of Baskerville investigates a puzzling series of murders. / Bruder William von Baskerville versucht, eine Reihe rätselhafter Morde aufzuklären. / Le frère William de Baskerville enquête sur une étrange série de meurtres.

« Je suis acteur. Ce n'est pas de la chirurgie cérébrale. Si je fais bien mon boulot, les gens ne demanderont pas à être remboursés. »
Sean Connery

exigences de la mode. Malgré la franchise parfois surprenante de Connery – annonçant par exemple son départ en retraite par ces mots : « J'en ai marre des idiots, du fossé toujours plus grand entre les gens qui savent faire des films et ceux qui les financent » –, ses confrères louent invariablement sa sincérité, mais aussi son altruisme et sa modestie.

Connery se moque de l'histoire de sa propre vie : « On pourrait croire que j'ai pris de grandes décisions spectaculaires, mais en fait, non. J'ai sans doute eu la vocation dès le départ, [...] mais mes ambitions étaient bien en deçà. » À l'instar de la plupart des artistes qui ont acquis une reconnaissance mondiale, Connery ne peut que reconnaître sa volonté de réussir. Contrairement à la grande majorité d'entre eux, il ne prétend pas avoir été prédestiné à la gloire, certain que son talent finirait par éblouir le monde. Il reconnaît seulement : « Je ne suis peut-être pas un bon acteur, mais je serais encore moins bon dans un autre boulot. »

Intuitif, comme beaucoup d'acteurs, d'écrivains et de réalisateurs, Connery rechigne à revendiquer les ficelles de son métier. Tout juste admet-il qu'à l'époque des petits rôles et des troupes ambulantes, dans les années 1950, il passait la plupart de son temps libre dans les bibliothèques municipales, à lire les grandes pièces classiques. Peu après arriverait Bond, James Bond. Inutile de rappeler comment Connery a exploité cette opportunité. Est-ce Bond qui a fait de lui une « authentique star du cinéma » ? Sans conteste. Est-ce la manière dont Connery a incarné Bond qui a jeté les bases de la franchise la plus populaire de l'histoire du cinéma ? C'est indiscutable. Ensemble, Bond et Connery ont pris une envergure mondiale ; mais c'est Connery, et non Bond, qui, par sa formidable présence, a imprégné une pléiade de rôles futurs. « Les temps changent, les styles évoluent », nota le réalisateur Terry Gilliam. « Sean ne change pas : il sait jouer tous les rôles, et il est toujours écossais. » Connery peut être aussi décontracté et charismatique que Steve McQueen, aussi élégant que Katharine Hepburn ou aussi généreux que Frank Sinatra. La seule chose qu'il ne puisse être, c'est anglais, parce que cela serait faux. Un de ses deux tatouages clame « Scotland Forever » et Connery a été anobli par la Reine d'Angleterre malgré son fervent nationalisme écossais.

Connery possède la sincérité profonde qui le rend « authentique » aux yeux de Spielberg et de quantité d'autres artistes avec lesquels il a travaillé. En existe-t-il six autres comme lui ? Pas d'après une autre Hepburn, Audrey, qui fut sa partenaire d'un film et affirma : « Il n'existe à mon avis que deux grandes stars qui n'ont pas été changées par leur immense succès : Sean Connery et Lassie. »

PAGES 24/25
STILL FROM
'REQUIEM FOR A HEAVYWEIGHT' (1957)
Connery's best work in the early years was for television. His big break was replacing Jack Palance as Mountain McClintock in a live broadcast of Rod Serling's script. / In seiner frühen Karriere lieferte Connery seine beste Arbeit im Fernsehen ab. Den großen Durchbruch erlebte er in der Rolle von Mountain McClintock in einem Live-Fernsehspiel nach einem Drehbuch von Rod Serling. / Connery connaît ses premiers succès à la télévision. La chance lui sourit lorsqu'il remplace Jack Palance dans le rôle de Mountain McClintock dans ce téléfilm d'après un scénario de Rod Serling.

OPPOSITE/RECHTS/PAGE CI-CONTRE
PORTRAIT (SEPTEMBER 1983)

PAGE 22
PORTRAIT (CIRCA 1953)
Bodybuilder Connery posed as a model for art students and magazines. / Bodybuilder Connery stand für Kunststudenten und Zeitschriften Modell. / Connery le culturiste posa comme modèle pour des étudiants en art et des magazines.

2

VISUAL FILMOGRAPHY

FILMOGRAFIE IN BILDERN

FILMOGRAPHIE EN IMAGES

STILL FROM 'HELL DRIVERS' (1957)
Bit parts in tough crime films allowed Connery to study and learn from powerful actors like Stanley Baker (on floor) and Patrick McGoohan (standing). / Kleine Nebenrollen in harten Kriminalfilmen gaben Connery Gelegenheit, starken Schauspielern wie Stanley Baker (am Boden) und Patrick McGoohan (stehend) auf die Finger zu schauen und von ihnen zu lernen. / Des petits rôles dans des films de gangsters permettent à Connery de se perfectionner au contact de comédiens confirmés comme Stanley Baker (au sol) et Patrick McGoohan (debout).

STILL FROM 'ACTION OF THE TIGER' (1957)
Sailor Mike (Connery) tries to seduce Tracy Malvoisie (Martine Carol) in this typical adventure story directed by Terence Young. / In dieser typischen Abenteuergeschichte unter der Regie von Terence Young versucht der Matrose Mike (Connery), Tracy Malvoisie (Martine Carol) zu verführen. / Mike le marin (Connery) tente de séduire Tracy Malvoisie (Martine Carol) dans ce film d'aventure classique dirigé par Terence Young.

**STILL FROM
'ANOTHER TIME, ANOTHER PLACE' (1958)**
Connery's first major film role, opposite Hollywood
movie star Lana Turner. Off screen, Connery had to
disarm Turner's jealous, gun-toting gangster boyfriend,
Johnny Stompanato. / Seine erste große Filmrolle
spielte Connery an der Seite von Hollywoodstar Lana
Turner. Hinter den Kulissen musste sich Connery gegen
Turners eifersüchtigen Freund, den schwer bewaffneten
Gangster Johnny Stompanato, zur Wehr setzen. /
Le premier grand rôle de Connery au cinéma, face à la
vedette de Hollywood Lana Turner. Hors écran,
Connery dut repousser les assauts du petit ami
gangster de la star, Johnny Stompanato, armé et
fort jaloux.

**STILL FROM
'TARZAN'S GREATEST ADVENTURE' (1959)**
Popcorn film work contrasted with Connery's serious,
literary TV and theater productions. / Connerys Rolle in
diesem „Popcornfilm" stand in starkem Gegensatz zu
seinen ernsthaften, literarischen Fernseh- und Theater-
rollen. / La participation de Connery à des films
« pop-corn » contraste avec son travail plus sérieux et
intellectuel pour la télévision ou le théâtre.

**STILL FROM 'DARBY O'GILL
AND THE LITTLE PEOPLE' (1959)**
Despite pleasant chats with Walt Disney every day,
Connery did not find the film artistically rewarding. /
Obwohl er sich jeden Tag nett mit Walt Disney
unterhielt, fühlte sich Connery von diesem Film
künstlerisch unterfordert. / Malgré d'agréables
conversations quotidiennes avec Walt Disney,
Connery jugea le film peu intéressant d'un point
de vue artistique.

**ON THE SET OF 'DARBY O'GILL
AND THE LITTLE PEOPLE' (1959)**
Michael McBride (Connery) romances Katie O'Gill
(Janet Munro)—Connery's song "Pretty Irish Girl" was
released as a single in the UK. / Michael McBride
(Connery) turtelt mit Katie O'Gill (Janet Munro).
Connerys Filmlied „Pretty Irish Girl" kam in Groß-
britannien sogar als Single auf den Markt. / Michael
McBride (Connery) charme Katie O'Gill (Janet Munro) ;
la chanson qu'interprète Connery, « Pretty Irish Girl »,
sortira en 45 tours au Royaume-Uni.

STILL FROM 'THE FRIGHTENED CITY' (1961)
Playing a rougher character, a thug with ethics, Paddy
Damion, here being interrogated by Sayers (John
Gregson). / Hier spielt er eine raubeinigere Figur: Paddy
Damion, einen Schläger mit Moral, der hier von Sayers
(John Gregson) verhört wird. / Dans un rôle plus dur,
celui du voyou sans morale Paddy Damion, interrogé ici
par Sayers (John Gregson).

STILL FROM 'THE FRIGHTENED CITY' (1961)
The rough-and-tumble action sequences allowed
Connery to show his physical expertise. / Die flotten
Actionszenen gaben Connery Gelegenheit, seine
körperlichen Fähigkeiten zur Schau zu stellen. / Les
séquences d'action chaotiques permettent à Connery
de démontrer son aisance physique.

STILL FROM 'ON THE FIDDLE' (1961)

Pedlar Pascoe (Connery) is just there to feed straight lines to Horace Pope (Alfred Lynch), but Connery's warmth makes the film watchable. / Pedlar Pascoe (Connery) ist nicht viel mehr als ein Stichwortgeber für Horace Pope (Alfred Lynch), aber Connerys Warmherzigkeit macht den Film sehenswert. / Pedlar Pascoe (Connery) n'est là que pour donner la réplique à Horace Pope (Alfred Lynch), mais c'est bien la chaleur de Connery qui rend ce film supportable.

"It reads as though one had made great dramatic decisions, but in fact one didn't. I certainly had the drive from the beginning, but the targets and ambitions were much, much less."
Sean Connery

„Es liest sich so, als habe jemand große dramatische Entscheidungen getroffen, aber in Wirklichkeit war dem nicht so. Ich besaß gewiss von Anfang an den Antrieb, aber die Ziele und Ambitionen waren sehr viel geringer."
Sean Connery

« On pourrait croire que j'ai pris de grandes décisions spectaculaires, mais en fait, non. J'ai sans doute eu la vocation dès le départ, mais mes ambitions étaient bien en deça. »
Sean Connery

STILL FROM 'THE LONGEST DAY' (1962)
Connery spent two days filming this re-creation of
the D-Day landings in France during World War II. /
Connery brauchte zwei Drehtage für seinen Auftritt
in dieser Nacherzählung der Ereignisse rund um die
Landung der Alliierten in der Normandie im Zweiten
Weltkrieg. / Connery a passé deux jours sur le tournage
de cette reconstitution du débarquement allié en
France pendant la Seconde Guerre mondiale.

"We'd never seen a surer guy or a more arrogant son of a bitch."
Harry Saltzman, producer

„Wir hatten noch nie einen selbstsichereren Typen oder einen arroganteren Hurensohn gesehen."
Harry Saltzman, Produzent

« On n'avait jamais vu un type aussi sûr de lui, un salaud aussi arrogant que lui. »
Harry Saltzman, producteur

"He's not what I envisioned. I'm looking for Commander Bond, not an overgrown stunt man."
Ian Fleming, writer

„Er ist nicht das, was ich mir vorgestellt hatte. Ich suche nach einem Commander Bond, nicht nach einem überwachsenen Stuntman."
Ian Fleming, Schriftsteller

« Il ne correspond pas à ce que j'avais imaginé. Je cherchais le commandant Bond, pas un cascadeur monté en graine. »
Ian Fleming, écrivain

PORTRAIT FOR 'DR. NO' (1962)
Posed with the trademark Walther PPK gun and vodka martini—presumably shaken, not stirred. / Hier posiert Connery mit seinen Markenzeichen: einer Pistole vom Typ Walther PPK und einem Wodka Martini - vermutlich geschüttelt, nicht gerührt. / Connery pose avec les fameux attributs de Bond : son Walther PPK et sa vodka martini - frappée et non remuée.

ON THE SET OF 'DR. NO' (1962)
Relaxing on set in Jamaica, where filming began on
January 16, 1962. / Eine Drehpause in Jamaika, wo am
16. Januar 1962 die Dreharbeiten begannen. / Détente en
Jamaïque, où le tournage a commencé le 16 janvier 1962.

STILL FROM 'DR. NO' (1962)
Director Terence Young dressed and molded the rough-
hewn Connery. / Regisseur Terence Young kleidete und
formte den grobschlächtigen Connery. / Le réalisateur
Terence Young habilla, façonna et dégrossit Connery.

"There's one major difference between James Bond and me. He is able to sort out problems!"
Sean Connery

„Es gibt einen großen Unterschied zwischen James Bond und mir. Er ist in der Lage, mit Problemen fertig zu werden!"
Sean Connery

« Il y a une différence majeure entre James Bond et moi. Il est capable de résoudre les problèmes ! »
Sean Connery

STILL FROM 'DR. NO' (1962)
Connery quickly established the hard-edged, cynical character who manhandled men and women alike. / Connery etablierte rasch die Figur des Zynikers mit harten Kanten, der Männer wie Frauen „in die Mangel" zu nehmen verstand. / Connery comprend vite comment camper ce personnage anguleux et cynique qui traite hommes et femmes avec la même sévérité.

ON THE SET OF 'DR. NO' (1962)
Ten days into filming, Connery and Ursula Andress were still unaware of the worldwide attention that the film would generate. / Nach zehn Drehtagen waren sich Connery und Ursula Andress noch immer nicht der Aufmerksamkeit bewusst, die der Film weltweit erregte. / Après dix jours de tournage, Connery et Ursula Andress ignorent encore l'intérêt mondial que va susciter le film.

ON THE SET OF 'DR. NO' (1962)
Actress Zena Marshall: "James Bond made him a walking aphrodisiac." / Schauspielerin Zena Marshall: „James Bond machte ihn zu einem wandelnden Aphrodisiakum." / L'actrice Zena Marshall : « James Bond a fait de lui un aphrodisiaque ambulant. »

ON THE SET OF 'DR. NO' (1962)

Connery was liked on the set because of his professionalism, his willingness to do his own stunts, and his sharp sense of humor. / Bei den Dreharbeiten war Connery wegen seiner Professionalität ebenso beliebt wie aufgrund seines bissigen Humors und seiner Bereitschaft, seine Stunts selbst zu drehen. / Connery était apprécié sur le plateau pour son professionnalisme, son sens de l'humour acide et sa volonté indéfectible d'exécuter lui-même ses propres cascades.

ON THE SET OF 'DR. NO' (1962)

Initially 007 creator Ian Fleming wanted an established actor with class to play James Bond, and was dismayed when Connery was cast. However, Fleming was won over by Connery and his performance, even using Connery as the basis for his later novels. / Ursprünglich wollte Ian Fleming, der Erfinder von „007", einen etablierten Schauspieler in der Rolle des James Bond sehen und war bestürzt, als sie mit Connery besetzt wurde. Connery konnte Fleming jedoch mit seiner Leistung überzeugen, woraufhin dieser seine Darstellung sogar zur Vorlage für die späteren Bond-Romane nahm. / À l'origine, le créateur de 007, Ian Fleming, souhaitait qu'un acteur confirmé et élégant incarne son James Bond, et fut très déçu quand Connery fut choisi. Fleming fut cependant séduit par Connery et sa prestation, au point qu'il s'inspira de lui pour ses romans ultérieurs.

PAGES 46/47
POSTER FOR
'FROM RUSSIA WITH LOVE' (1963)

JAMES BOND

BACK!

007

IAN FLEMING'S

FROM
RUSSIA
WITH
LOVE

TECHNICOLOR

**STILL FROM
'FROM RUSSIA WITH LOVE' (1963)**
The film is full of memorable characters. Here Rosa
Klebb (torch singer Lotte Lenya) attacks Bond with a
poisoned blade concealed in her shoe. / Der Film ist
vollgepackt mit unvergesslichen Figuren. Hier greift
Rosa Klebb (gespielt von der Sängerin Lotte Lenya)
Bond mit einem vergifteten Messer an, das in ihrem
Schuh versteckt war. / Le film regorge de personnages
mémorables. Ici, Rosa Klebb (la chanteuse Lotte Lenya)
attaque Bond avec une lame empoisonnée dissimulée
dans sa chaussure.

**STILL FROM
'FROM RUSSIA WITH LOVE' (1963)**
The films followed a familiar formula: In the first half,
Bond tries to find the villain; in the second half, Bond
tries to escape the villain's clutches. / Die Filme folgten
einem vertrauten Schema: In der ersten Hälfte versucht
Bond, den Bösewicht zu finden, und in der zweiten, sich
aus dessen Fängen zu befreien. / Les films suivent une
recette éprouvée : dans la première partie, Bond
cherche le méchant ; dans la seconde, Bond cherche à
lui échapper.

STILL FROM
'FROM RUSSIA WITH LOVE' (1963)
Red Grant (Robert Shaw) is a strong, implacable hit man
who will never give up. / Red Grant (Robert Shaw) ist
ein starker, unerbittlicher Auftragskiller, der niemals
aufgibt. / Red Grant (Robert Shaw) est un tueur à gages
puissant et implacable, qui n'abandonne jamais.

PAGES 52/53
STILL FROM
'FROM RUSSIA WITH LOVE' (1963)
In chases on land or on water, with Bond behind the
wheel or at the helm, there is often a beauty (here
Daniela Bianchi) at his side. / Bei diversen
Verfolgungsjagden zu Lande oder zu Wasser, stand
ihm oft eine Schönheit (in diesem Fall Daniela Bianchi)
zur Seite. / Dans les scènes de poursuites – sur terre
ou sur mer –, James Bond a souvent une beauté à ses
côtés (ici Daniela Bianchi).

STILL FROM
'FROM RUSSIA WITH LOVE' (1963)
The brutal fight between Grant and Bond is a template
for future Bond films. / Der brutale Kampf zwischen
Grant und Bond gab das Muster für spätere Bond-Filme
vor. / Le combat brutal entre Grant et Bond servira de
modèle pour les futurs films de la série.

STILL FROM 'WOMAN OF STRAW' (1964)
Tony Richmond (Connery) persuades Maria Marcello
(Gina Lollobrigida) to marry an invalid so that they can
steal his money. / Tony Richmond (Connery) überredet
Maria Marcello (Gina Lollobrigida), einen Invaliden zu
heiraten, um dann mit ihr dessen Geld zu stehlen. /
Tony Richmond (Connery) convainc Maria Marcello
(Gina Lollobrigida) d'épouser un invalide pour qu'ils
puissent ensemble lui voler son argent.

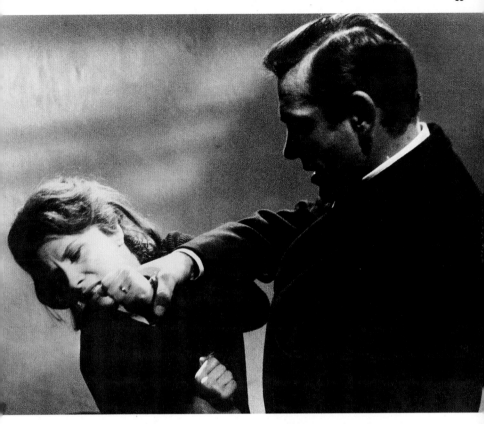

STILL FROM 'WOMAN OF STRAW' (1964)
Such is the intensity of his acting style, Connery accidentally hit Lollobrigida during the filming of this scene. / Connery war so in seine Rolle vertieft, dass er Lollobrigida bei den Dreharbeiten zu dieser Szene versehentlich verletzte. / Son jeu est si intense que Connery frappe accidentellement Lollobrigida pendant le tournage de cette scène.

"Love may not make the world go 'round, but I must admit that it makes the ride worthwhile."
Sean Connery

„Es mag sein, dass Liebe nicht die Welt in Gang hält, aber ich muss zugeben: Sie sorgt dafür, dass sich die Fahrt lohnt."
Sean Connery

« L'amour ne fait peut-être pas tourner le monde, mais je dois admettre qu'il rend le voyage intéressant. »
Sean Connery

STILL FROM 'MARNIE' (1964)
Mark Rutland tells thief Marnie (Tippi Hedren): "I've
caught you and, by god, I'm going to keep you." / Mark
Rutland lässt die Diebin Marnie (Tippi Hedren) wissen:
„Ich hab dich gefangen, und ich schwöre dir: Ich werde
dich auch behalten." / Mark Rutland à la voleuse Marnie
(Tippi Hedren): «Je vous ai attrapée et, Dieu m'en soit
témoin, je vais vous garder.»

STILL FROM 'MARNIE' (1964)
Director Alfred Hitchcock liked Connery's relaxed
attitude and lack of star ego. / Regisseur Alfred
Hitchcock gefiel es, dass Connery so entspannt war
und keine Starallüren besaß. / Le réalisateur Alfred
Hitchcock aimait l'attitude détendue de Connery, ainsi
que son humilité.

STILL FROM 'GOLDFINGER' (1964)
The production traveled to Switzerland and America
for location work, but, as usual, most of the production
was filmed in the UK. / Ein Teil der Dreharbeiten fand
in der Schweiz und in Amerika statt, aber wie üblich
wurde der größte Teil des Films in Großbritannien
gedreht. / La production se déplace en Suisse et aux
États-Unis pour des scènes en décors naturels mais,
comme toujours, le tournage a principalement lieu au
Royaume-Uni.

PORTRAIT FOR 'GOLDFINGER' (1964)
In a reflective moment, leaning on the fender of the
specially equipped Aston Martin. / In einem kurzen
Augenblick der Nachdenklichkeit lehnt sich Bond an
den Kotflügel seines speziell ausgestatteten Aston
Martin. / Un moment de réflexion, appuyé contre l'aile
de son Aston Martin spécialement équipée.

"There is nothing like a challenge to bring out the best in a man."
Sean Connery

„Nichts ist hilfreicher als eine Herausforderung, um das Beste in einem Menschen hervorzubringen."
Sean Connery

« Rien de tel qu'un défi pour faire ressortir le meilleur d'un homme. »
Sean Connery

STILL FROM 'GOLDFINGER' (1964)
Goldfinger (Gert Fröbe) proved to be more techno-logically advanced than previous Bond antagonists. / Goldfinger (Gert Fröbe) war technisch fortschrittlicher als Bonds frühere Gegenspieler. / Goldfinger (Gert Fröbe) utilise une technologie plus perfectionnée que les précédents adversaires de Bond.

PAGE 62
PORTRAIT FOR 'GOLDFINGER' (1964)
Connery resented all the money his producers were making from his work, so he negotiated $50,000 and a percentage for his third Bond film. / Connery ärgerte sich über die Profite, die seine Produzenten aus den Filmen schlugen, und so handelte er für seinen dritten Bond-Film zu seiner Gage von 50.000 US-Dollar eine Gewinnbeteiligung aus. / Connery n'apprécie pas que ses producteurs gagnent autant d'argent grâce à son travail ; il négocie une prime de 50 000 dollars et un pourcentage sur les bénéfices du troisième opus de la franchise James Bond.

PAGE 63
STILL FROM 'GOLDFINGER' (1964)
Bond is tossed around Fort Knox by the thuggish Odd Job (Harold Sakata). / In Fort Knox wird Bond von dem Schlägertypen Odd Job (Harold Sakata) durch die Gegend gewirbelt. / Bond est malmené à travers Fort Knox par le malfrat Oddjob (Harold Sakata).

STILL FROM 'GOLDFINGER' (1964)
The lesbian aspect of Pussy Galore (Honor Blackman)
was toned down for the film. / Dass Pussy Galore
(Honor Blackman) lesbisch war, wurde in der Verfilmung
heruntergespielt. / La facette lesbienne de Pussy
Galore (Honor Blackman) fut atténuée pour le film.

STILL FROM 'GOLDFINGER' (1964)
Goldfinger's secretary, Jill Masterton (Shirley Eaton),
falls for Bond and betrays her boss. / Goldfingers
Sekretärin Jill Masterton (Shirley Eaton) verliebt sich in
Bond und verrät ihren Chef. / La secrétaire de
Goldfinger, Jill Masterton (Shirley Eaton), tombe
amoureuse de Bond et trahit son patron.

PAGES 66/67
STILL FROM 'GOLDFINGER' (1964)
Auric Goldfinger revenges himself by gilding Jill's body,
creating one of filmdom's most memorable images. /
Auric Goldfinger rächt sich, indem er Jills Körper mit
Gold überzieht und damit eines der denkwürdigsten
Bilder der Filmgeschichte schafft. / Auric Goldfinger se
venge en recouvrant d'or le corps de Jill, créant une des
images les plus célèbres du cinéma.

STILL FROM 'THUNDERBALL' (1965)
In the pre-credits sequence, Bond is attacked by the widow of a SPECTRE spy. / In der Sequenz, die dem Vorspann vorausgeht, wird Bond von der „Witwe" eines SPECTRE-Spions angegriffen. / Dans la séquence de prégénérique, Bond est attaqué par la veuve d'un espion du SPECTRE.

PAGES 68/69
STILL FROM 'THE HILL' (1965)
Connery finally got some acting accolades when he portrayed the oft-disciplined Joe Roberts for director Sidney Lumet. / Für seine Darstellung des mehrfach disziplinarisch gemaßregelten Joe Roberts unter der Regie von Sidney Lumet fand Connerys schauspielerisches Talent endlich Würdigung. / Connery reçoit enfin des louanges pour son jeu lorsqu'il incarne la forte tête Joe Roberts pour le réalisateur Sidney Lumet.

STILL FROM 'THUNDERBALL' (1965)
The widow turns out to be the spy Bond was looking for. / Es stellt sich heraus, dass die Witwe jener Spion ist, nach dem Bond suchte. / La veuve s'avère être l'espion que Bond recherchait.

PAGES 72 & 73
STILLS FROM 'THUNDERBALL' (1965)
Bond makes his escape with a jet pack. Connery, long tired of Bond's compressed range of emotion, wanted to escape the character. / Bond flieht mit einem Raketenrucksack. Connery war der begrenzten emotionalen Bandbreite der Figur langsam überdrüssig und wollte sich von Bond lösen. / Bond parvient à s'enfuir grâce à un jetpack. Connery, déjà fatigué de l'éventail émotionnel restreint que lui offre Bond, voudrait aussi échapper à son personnage.

STILL FROM 'THUNDERBALL' (1965)
The film shows Bond's pursuit of two missing nuclear
warheads, and he needs the help of Domino (Claudine
Auger) to find them. / Der Film zeigt, wie Bond zwei
abhandengekommenen Nuklearsprengköpfen nachjagt;
um sie zu finden, bedient er sich der Hilfe von Domino
(Claudine Auger). / Dans ce film, Bond est à la recherche
de deux têtes nucléaires disparues ; pour les trouver, il
doit s'aider de Domino (Claudine Auger).

OPPOSITE/RECHTS/PAGE CI-CONTRE
ON THE SET OF 'THUNDERBALL' (1965)

PAGE 76
ON THE SET OF 'THUNDERBALL' (1965)

PAGE 77
POSTER ART FOR 'THUNDERBALL' (1965)

STILL FROM 'A FINE MADNESS' (1966)
Samson Shillitoe (Connery) is depressed because he
cannot finish his epic poem, so Rhoda (Joanne
Woodward) pays for a psychiatrist to cure him. /
Samson Shillitoe (Connery) leidet unter Depressionen,
weil er sein Gedichtepos nicht vollenden kann, also
engagiert Rhoda (Joanne Woodward) einen Psychiater,
der ihm helfen soll. / Samson Shillitoe (Connery) est
déprimé parce qu'il ne parvient pas à terminer son
poème épique ; Rhoda (Joanne Woodward) paie alors
un psychiatre pour le guérir.

STILL FROM 'A FINE MADNESS' (1966)
Connery greatly enjoyed making this comedy with so
many fine actors. / Connery machte es großen Spaß,
dieses Lustspiel mit vielen talentierten Kollegen und
Kolleginnen drehen zu können. / Connery prit un
grand plaisir à tourner cette comédie avec tant de
bons acteurs.

"My dear girl, don't flatter yourself. What I did this evening was for queen and country. You don't think it gave me any pleasure, do you?"
James Bond, *Thunderball* (1965)

„Mein liebes Mädchen, bilde dir nur nichts ein. Was ich heute Abend getan habe, war für Königin und Vaterland. Du glaubst doch nicht etwa, es habe mir Spaß gemacht, oder?"
James Bond, *Feuerball* (1965)

« Ma chère petite, ne vous flattez pas. Ce que j'ai fait ce soir, je l'ai fait pour la reine et mon pays. Vous ne croyez tout de même pas que j'en ai éprouvé du plaisir, n'est-ce pas ? »
James Bond, *Opération Tonnerre* (1965)

POSTER ART FOR 'YOU ONLY LIVE TWICE' (1967)

The Bond films were becoming more absurd, with more exotic locations, bigger sets, and more gadgets. This was the last of Connery's five contracted Bond films. / Die Bond-Filme wurden immer absurder, die Schauplätze exotischer, die Kulissen größer und das technische Spielzeug umfangreicher. Dies war der letzte der fünf Bond-Filme, zu denen sich Connery vertraglich verpflichtet hatte. / Les James Bond deviennent de plus en plus absurdes, les lieux de tournages de plus en plus exotiques, les équipes s'étoffent et les gadgets se multiplient. Ce cinquième épisode est le dernier pour lequel Connery est lié par contrat.

PAGES 82 & 83
STILLS FROM 'YOU ONLY LIVE TWICE' (1967)

Always happy to take on physical challenges, Connery learned and mastered martial arts for the fight sequences. / Connery freute sich, wie immer, über körperliche Herausforderungen und lernte für die Kampfszenen dieses Films fernöstliche Kampfkunst, bis er sie beherrschte. / Toujours ravi de relever les défis physiques, Connery apprend à maîtriser les arts martiaux pour les scènes de combat.

ON THE SET OF
'YOU ONLY LIVE TWICE' (1967)
Ken Adam's incredible set designs were the largest yet made for a Bond film. / Die gewaltigen Kulissen, die Ken Adam entwarf, waren zur damaligen Zeit die größten, die je für einen Bond-Film gebaut wurden. / Les incroyables décors de Ken Adam sont alors les plus grands jamais conçus pour un James Bond.

LEFT/LINKS/CI-CONTRE
STILL FROM 'YOU ONLY LIVE TWICE' (1967)
Bond is required to disguise himself to infiltrate the Japanese hideout. / Bond muss sich verkleiden, um in das japanische Versteck einzudringen. / Bond doit se déguiser pour infiltrer une planque japonaise.

PAGES 86/87
STILL FROM 'YOU ONLY LIVE TWICE' (1967)
There was never any question that Bond would again derail the villain's plan to rule the world. / Es gab zu keinem Zeitpunkt wirkliche Zweifel daran, dass Bond auch diesmal wieder die Pläne des Bösewichts zur Erlangung der Weltherrschaft durchkreuzen würde. / Il ne fait aucun doute que Bond parviendra une fois de plus à déjouer les plans du méchant pour contrôler le monde.

STILLS FROM 'YOU ONLY LIVE TWICE' (1967)

Bond's on-screen calm was in contrast with Connery's displeasure with both the producers and the constant harassment of the press. / Bonds Gelassenheit vor der Kamera stand in krassem Gegensatz zu Connerys Missmut über die Produzenten und über die ständige Belästigung durch die Presse. / Le flegme qu'affiche Bond à l'écran contraste avec l'agacement que ressent Connery à l'égard de ses producteurs et de la presse, laquelle ne cesse de le harceler.

STILL FROM 'SHALAKO' (1968)
Since he was a child in Fountainbridge, Edinburgh,
Connery always dreamed of being in a western. Here
Shalako (Connery) fights Chato (Woody Strode). /
Seit seiner Kindheit im Edinburgher Stadtteil
Fountainbridge hatte Connery davon geträumt, in
einem Western mitzuspielen. Hier kämpft Shalako
(Connery) mit Chato (Woody Strode). / Depuis son
enfance dans le quartier de Fountainbridge, à
Édimbourg, Connery a toujours rêvé de jouer dans un
Western. Ici, Shalako (Connery) se bat contre Chato
(Woody Strode).

*"I admit I'm being paid well, but it's no more than I
deserve. After all, I've been screwed more times
than a hooker."*
Sean Connery

*„Ich gebe zu, dass ich gut bezahlt werde, aber es
ist nicht mehr, als mir zusteht. Schließlich bin ich
öfter gefickt worden als eine Nutte."*
Sean Connery

*« J'admets que je suis bien payé, mais pas plus que
je ne le mérite. Après tout, je me suis fait baiser
plus souvent qu'une putain. »*
Sean Connery

STILL FROM 'SHALAKO' (1968)
There was little chemistry between Connery and costar
Brigitte Bardot, who was constantly late and threatened
to leave the production before it was finished. /
Connery verstand sich nicht sonderlich gut mit seiner
Kollegin Brigitte Bardot, die ständig zu spät kam und
drohte, die Dreharbeiten zu verlassen, bevor der Film
fertig war. / Le courant passe mal entre Connery et sa
partenaire Brigitte Bardot qui, perpétuellement en
retard, menace de quitter le tournage avant qu'il ne
soit terminé.

"More than anything else, I'd like to be an old man with a good face, like Hitchcock or Picasso."
Sean Connery

„Ich möchte vor allem ein alter Mann mit einem guten Gesicht sein, so wie Hitchcock oder Picasso."
Sean Connery

« Plus que tout, j'aimerais être un vieil homme avec une bonne tête, comme Hitchcock ou Picasso. »
Sean Connery

**STILL FROM 'THE RED TENT'
('KRASNAYA PALATKA', 1969)**
Roald Amundsen (Connery) leads a rescue party to a crashed dirigible in the Arctic. The rescue failed, and so did the film. / Roald Amundsen (Connery) führt die Rettungsmannschaft zu einem in der Arktis abgestürzten Luftschiff. Dem Film war das gleiche Schicksal beschieden wie der Rettungsaktion. / Roald Amundsen (Connery) guide un groupe de secouristes jusqu'à un dirigeable échoué dans l'Arctique. L'opération échoue, le film aussi.

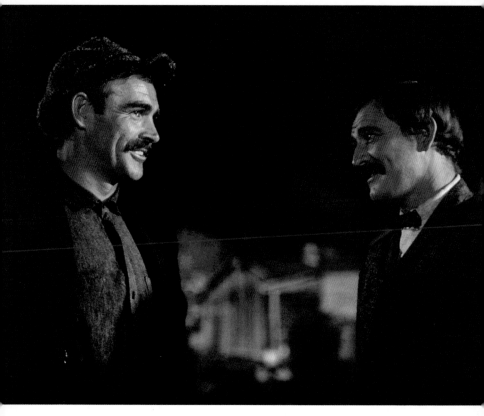

STILL FROM 'THE MOLLY MAGUIRES' (1970)
Jack Kehoe (Connery) leads a secret army of Irish
miners who take murderous revenge on their
employers. A spy, James McKenna (Richard Harris),
joins the group, in this film based on a true story. / In
diesem Film, der auf einer wahren Begebenheit beruht,
führt Jack Kehoe (Connery) eine Geheimarmee irischer
Bergarbeiter an, die sich auf mörderische Weise an
ihren Arbeitgebern rächen. James McKenna (Richard
Harris) wird als Spion in die Gruppe eingeschleust. /
Jack Kehoe (Connery) dirige une milice secrète de
mineurs irlandais qui se vengent violemment de leurs
patrons. Un espion, James McKenna (Richard Harris),
infiltre le groupe. Le film s'inspire d'une histoire vraie.

"You're a cool one. I have no coolness in me at all."
Jack Kehoe, *The Molly Maguires* (1970)

*„Du bist ein cooler Typ. In mir steckt überhaupt
nichts Cooles."*
Jack Kehoe, *Verflucht bis zum jüngsten Tag* (1970)

*« Toi, tu es du genre calme. Moi je n'ai rien
de calme. »*
Jack Kehoe, *Traître sur commande* (1970)

STILL FROM 'THE MOLLY MAGUIRES' (1970)
Connery is always best when playing a man of the
people. However, the film was a huge flop and Connery
needed a hit to establish himself as a moneymaking star
outside of the James Bond franchise. / Connery ist
immer dann in Höchstform, wenn er einen Mann aus
dem Volk spielt. Der Film war allerdings ein gewaltiger
Flop, und Connery brauchte dringend einen Erfolg,
um der Welt zu zeigen, dass er auch außerhalb der
James-Bond-Filme Geld an den Kinokassen einspielen
konnte. / Connery est toujours meilleur quand il incarne
un homme du peuple. Mais le film est un four et
Connery a besoin d'un succès pour se remettre en selle
et retrouver son statut de vedette rentable hors de la
franchise James Bond.

ON THE SET OF
'THE ANDERSON TAPES' (1971)

Connery reteamed with director Sidney Lumet (center)
to make a heist movie in New York City with Dyan
Cannon. / Connery tat sich wieder mit Regisseur Sidney
Lumet (Mitte) zusammen, um mit Dyan Cannon diesen
Film über einen Raubüberfall in New York City zu
drehen. / Connery fait à nouveau équipe avec le
réalisateur Sidney Lumet (au centre) pour une histoire
de cambriolage située à New York, avec Dyan Cannon.

"It's just dog-eat-dog, but I want the first bite."
John "Duke" Anderson, *The Anderson Tapes* (1971)

„Es ist so, dass ein Hund den anderen frisst, aber
ich will den ersten Biss haben."
John „Duke" Anderson, *Der Anderson-Clan* (1971)

« L'homme est un loup pour l'homme, mais je
mordrai le premier. »
John « Duke » Anderson, *Le Gang Anderson* (1971)

**STILL FROM
'THE ANDERSON TAPES' (1971)**
The tense, gritty action, the interplay of the characters,
and the ironic storytelling made this film a hit. / Die
packende und aktionsreiche Handlung, das Wechselspiel der Charaktere und die ironische Erzählweise
machten diesen Film zum Kassenschlager. / Une
intrigue dense et agressive, une puissante interaction
entre les personnages et une narration pleine d'ironie
font de ce film un succès.

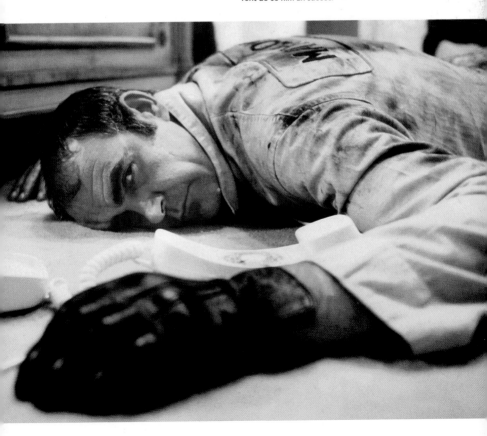

**STILL FROM
'DIAMONDS ARE FOREVER' (1971)**
The film verged on self-parody at times, as the
situations became more absurd and grotesque. /
Der Film grenzte streckenweise an eine Selbstparodie
mit immer absurderen und groteskeren Situationen. /
Le film frôle parfois l'autoparodie, à mesure que les
situations deviennent plus absurdes et grotesques.

**STILL FROM
'DIAMONDS ARE FOREVER' (1971)**
After accepting $1.2 million and a percentage of the
profits, Connery returned for a sixth James Bond film.
Here he suffers in a bout with Thumper (Trina Parks). /
Für 1,2 Millionen US-Dollar und eine Gewinnbeteiligung
ließ sich Connery auf einen sechsten James-Bond-Film
ein. Hier leidet er gerade im Zweikampf mit Thumper
(Trina Parks). / Connery accepte le cachet d'1,2 million
de dollars accompagné d'un pourcentage sur les
bénéfices et rempile pour un sixième James Bond.
Il subit ici l'attaque de Thumper (Trina Parks).

*"I've smelled that aftershave before, and both
times, I've smelled a rat."*
James Bond, *Diamonds Are Forever* (1971)

*„Ihr Aftershave habe ich schon mal irgendwo
gerochen, und beide Male sah ich eine Ratte."*
James Bond, *Diamantenfieber* (1971)

*« Bonjour, j'étais en train de promener mon rat, et je
me suis égaré. »*
James Bond, *Les diamants sont éternels* (1971)

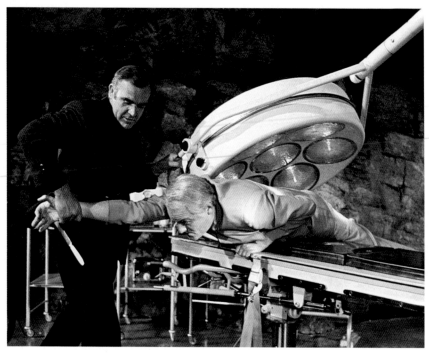

**STILL FROM
'DIAMONDS ARE FOREVER' (1971)**
But Bond could still turn the tables on his regular
nemesis, Ernst Stavro Blofeld (Charles Gray). /
Aber Bond schaffte es immer noch, seinen Erzrivalen
Ernst Stavro Blofeld (Charles Gray) über den Tisch
zu ziehen. / Mais Bond aura encore le dessus sur
son ennemi de toujours, Ernst Stavro Blofeld
(Charles Gray).

**STILL FROM
'DIAMONDS ARE FOREVER' (1971)**
One of the recurring motifs of the film: the attempts of
two offbeat assassins to kill Bond. Here Mr. Wint (Bruce
Glover) has a go. / Eines der immer wiederkehrenden
Motive des Films: Zwei schräge Mordbuben versuchen,
Bond zu töten. Hier ist Mr. Wint (Bruce Glover) an der
Reihe. / Un des motifs récurrents du film : deux tueurs
excentriques tentent d'assassiner Bond. Ici, c'est Wint
(Bruce Glover) qui tente sa chance.

**STILL FROM
'DIAMONDS ARE FOREVER' (1971)**
This is an in-joke—Connery is a keen golfer and plays
all over the world. In the end, the zany quality of the
film showed the future direction of the series. / Ein
Insiderwitz: Connery ist ein leidenschaftlicher Golfer
und spielt auf allen Plätzen der Welt. Letztendlich
zeigte die Albernheit des Films, in welche Richtung
sich die Reihe künftig bewegen würde. / Un clin d'œil :
Connery, grand amateur de golf, a joué sur les parcours
du monde entier. Le caractère loufoque du film montre
la voie qu'empruntera dès lors la série.

**ON THE SET OF
'DIAMONDS ARE FOREVER' (1971)**
Connery relaxes with costar Jill St. John. / Connery
entspannt sich mit seiner Kollegin Jill St. John. /
Moment de détente entre Connery et sa partenaire
à l'écran, Jill St. John.

STILL FROM 'THE OFFENCE' (1973)
In one of his greatest performances, unfairly buried by
United Artists at the time, Connery plays Detective
Sergeant Johnson, who is slowly and inexorably
corrupted by the nature of his job. / Connery lieferte
eine seiner besten schauspielerischen Leistungen in
diesem Film, den United Artists damals unfairerweise
unter den Tisch fallen ließ: Er spielt den Kripobeamten
Detective Sergeant Johnson, der allmählich, aber
unaufhaltsam vom Wesen seiner Arbeit korrumpiert
wird. / Dans un de ses plus grands rôles, à l'époque
injustement enterré par United Artists, Connery joue le
lieutenant Johnson, corrompu par la nature de son
métier de façon lente et inexorable.

STILL FROM 'THE OFFENCE' (1973)
As directed by Sidney Lumet, Connery comes to
believe that Kenneth Baxter (Ian Bannen) is the child
rapist they are searching for. Bannen was heavily
padded to protect himself from Connery's murderous
blows. / Unter der Regie von Sidney Lumet kommt
Johnson zu dem Schluss, dass Kenneth Baxter (Ian
Bannen) der gesuchte Kinderschänder sei. Bannen war
dick abgepolstert worden, um ihn vor Connerys
heftigen Schlägen zu schützen. / Sous la direction de
Sidney Lumet, Connery en vient à penser que Kenneth
Baxter (Ian Bannen) est le violeur d'enfants qu'ils
recherchent. Bannen était protégé par du molleton
pour encaisser les assauts violents de Connery.

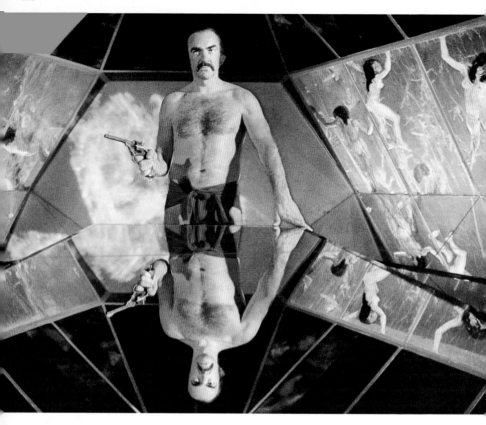

STILL FROM 'ZARDOZ' (1974)
In a film written and directed by John Boorman, Zed
(Connery) is a brutal exterminator in a postapocalyptic
world. / In diesem Film nach dem Buch und unter der
Regie von John Boorman ist Zed (Connery) ein brutaler
Ausrotter in einer postapokalyptischen Welt. / Dans ce
film écrit et réalisé par John Boorman, Zed (Connery)
est un exterminateur brutal dans un monde post-
apocalyptique.

"Some age, others mature."
Sean Connery

„Manche Leute altern, andere reifen."
Sean Connery

« Certains vieillissent, d'autres mûrissent. »
Sean Connery

STILL FROM 'ZARDOZ' (1974)
Connery read the script over a weekend, accepted the role, and within days was sitting down with John Boorman in Ireland to go through the script. / Connery las das Drehbuch an einem Wochenende, nahm die Rolle an und setzte sich ein paar Tage später mit John Boorman in Irland an einen Tisch, um das Buch durchzuarbeiten. / Connery lut le scénario en un week-end, accepta le rôle, et quelques jours plus tard, s'attablait avec John Boorman en Irlande pour travailler le script.

STILL FROM 'ZARDOZ' (1974)
As Zed becomes more civilized, the elite become more human. / Während Zed immer zivilisierter wird, wird die Elite menschlicher. / À mesure que Zed se civilise, l'élite s'humanise.

STILL FROM 'ZARDOZ' (1974)
Zed pierces the bubble of the Vortex elite, who are perfect and ageless. He brings aggression, hate, and passion into their world. / Zed lässt die Seifenblase der vollkommenen und alterslosen Vortex-Elite platzen, indem er Aggression, Hass und Leidenschaft in deren Welt bringt. / Zed perce la bulle dans laquelle vit l'élite Vortex, composée d'individus sans âge ni défauts. Il apporte l'agressivité, la haine et la passion dans leur monde.

"You stink of despair. Fight back. Fight for death, if that's what you want."
Zed, *Zardoz* (1974)

„Du stinkst nach Verzweiflung. Schlag zurück! Kämpfe um den Tod, wenn du ihn dir so sehr wünschst!"
Zed, *Zardoz* (1974)

« Tu pues le désespoir. Défends-toi. Bats-toi pour la mort, si c'est ce que tu souhaites. »
Zed, *Zardoz* (1974)

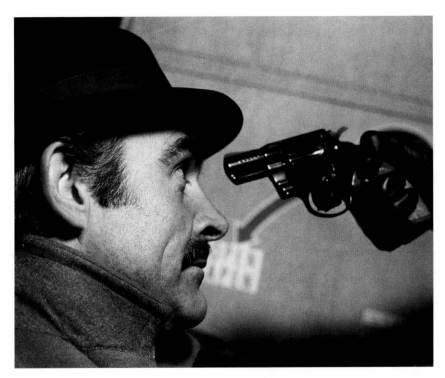

**STILL FROM 'THE TERRORISTS'
(AKA 'RANSOM', 1975)**
Colonel Tahlvik (Connery) is a security chief trying to
outwit a terrorist group holding an aircraft hostage. /
Colonel Tahlvik (Connery) ist ein Sicherheitschef, der
eine Flugzeugentführung zu vereiteln versucht. / Le
colonel Tahlvik (Connery) est un chef de la sécurité qui
tente de déjouer un détournement d'avion.

"Miss Debenham is not a woman. She is a lady."
Colonel Arbuthnot, *Murder on the Orient Express* (1974)

„Miss Debenham ist keine Frau. Sie ist eine Dame."
Colonel Arbuthnot, *Mord im Orient-Express* (1974)

*« Miss Debenham n'est pas une femme,
c'est une dame. »*
Colonel Arbuthnot, *Le Crime de l'Orient-Express* (1974)

**STILL FROM
'MURDER ON THE ORIENT EXPRESS' (1974)**
Colonel Arbuthnot (Connery) and his lover Mary
Debenham (Vanessa Redgrave) in director Sidney
Lumet's version of the Agatha Christie novel. / Colonel
Arbuthnot (Connery) und seine Geliebte Mary
Debenham (Vanessa Redgrave) in Sidney Lumets
Version des gleichnamigen Agatha-Christie-Romans. /
Le colonel Arbuthnot (Connery) et sa maîtresse, Mary
Debenham (Vanessa Redgrave), dans l'adaptation du
roman d'Agatha Christie signée Sidney Lumet.

STILL FROM 'THE WIND AND THE LION' (1975)
Mulay el-Raisuli (Connery) takes Eden Pedecaris
(Candice Bergen) and her children hostage in early
1900s Morocco. / Mulay el-Raisuli (Connery) nimmt
Eden Pedecaris (Candice Bergen) und ihre Kinder im
Marokko des frühen 20. Jahrhunderts als Geiseln. /
Mulay el-Raisuli (Connery) prend en otage Eden
Pedecaris (Candice Bergen) et ses enfants dans le
Maroc du début du XXe siècle.

STILL FROM 'THE WIND AND THE LION' (1975)
The dogmatic yet sympathetic chieftain inspired
renewed acting verve from Connery. / Durch die Rolle
des dogmatischen und doch sympathischen Stammes-
häuptlings fand Connery zu seinem schauspielerischen
Elan zurück. / Connery l'acteur trouve une verve
nouvelle dans ce personnage de chef de clan
dogmatique mais attachant.

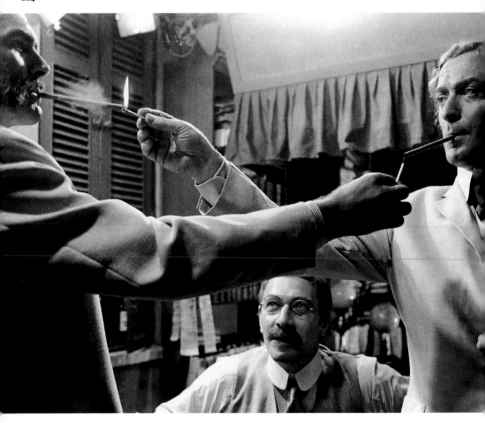

**STILL FROM
'THE MAN WHO WOULD BE KING' (1975)**
Danny Dravot (Connery) and Peachy Carnehan
(Michael Caine) are two British ex-soldiers who tell
Rudyard Kipling (Christopher Plummer, center) of their
plan to become rulers of a country. / Danny Dravot
(Connery) und Peachy Carnehan (Michael Caine) sind
zwei ehemalige britische Soldaten, die dem Schriftsteller Rudyard Kipling (Christopher Plummer, Mitte)
von ihrem Plan erzählen, Herrscher über ein Land zu
werden. / Danny Dravot (Connery) et Peachy Carnehan
(Michael Caine), deux vétérans britanniques, racontent
à Rudyard Kipling (Christopher Plummer, au centre)
comment ils comptent prendre la tête d'un pays.

*"Working with Danny [Connery] and Peachy
[Caine] was like watching a polished vaudeville
act—everything on cue, with perfect timing.
In fact with Sean Connery and Michael Caine,
there was not one conversation between us.
They just did it themselves."*
John Huston, director

**STILL FROM
'THE MAN WHO WOULD BE KING' (1975)**
In a script that director John Huston had originally developed for Humphrey Bogart and Clark Gable, Danny and Peachy achieve their dream. / Nach dem Drehbuch, das Regisseur John Huston ursprünglich für Humphrey Bogart und Clark Gable geschrieben hatte, erfüllen Danny und Peachy ihren Traum. / Dans ce script, que le réalisateur avait conçu au départ pour Humphrey Bogart et Clark Gable, Danny et Peachy réalisent leur rêve.

„Mit Danny [Connery] und Peachy [Caine] zu arbeiten war, als schaute man sich eine eingespielte Varieténummer an - alles klappte aufs Stichwort, das Timing war perfekt. Tatsächlich gab es beim Dreh mit Sean Connery und Michael Caine überhaupt keine Gespräche zwischen uns. Sie machten alles selbst."
John Huston, Regisseur

« Travailler avec Danny [Connery] et Peachy [Caine], c'était comme assister à un vaudeville bien rodé - chaque réplique tombait à point, avec un enchaînement parfait. En fait, il n'y a eu aucune conversation entre Sean Connery, Michael Caine et moi. Ils faisaient tout d'eux-mêmes. »
John Huston, réalisateur

"You are going to become soldiers. A soldier does not think. He only obeys. Do you really think that if a soldier thought twice he'd give his life for queen and country? Not bloody likely."
Daniel Dravot, *The Man Who Would Be King* (1975)

„Ihr werdet Soldaten. Ein Soldat denkt nicht. Er gehorcht nur. Glaubt ihr wirklich, wenn ein Soldat nachdächte, gäbe er sein Leben für Königin und Vaterland? Verdammt unwahrscheinlich!"
Daniel Dravot, *Der Mann, der König sein wollte* (1975)

« Vous allez devenir des soldats. Un soldat ne pense pas. Il se contente d'obéir. Vous croyez vraiment que s'il y réfléchissait à deux fois un soldat donnerait sa vie pour la Reine et le pays ? Aucun risque que ça arrive. »
Daniel Dravot, *L'Homme qui voulait être roi* (1975)

STILL FROM
'THE MAN WHO WOULD BE KING' (1975)
The monks believe that Danny is a god, and he becomes ruler of Kafiristan. This quality production was an enormous hit and established Connery as a money-making star outside of the Bond series. / Die Mönche halten Danny für einen Gott, und er wird Herrscher von Kafiristan. Dieser hochwertigen Produktion war ein gewaltiger Erfolg beschieden, der ein für alle Mal bewies, dass Connery auch außerhalb der Bond-Reihe die Kinokassen klingeln lassen konnte. / Les moines prennent Danny pour un dieu et il devient le dirigeant du Kafiristan. Cette production de qualité est un succès énorme et assoit Connery dans son statut d'acteur « rentable ». L'après-James Bond a commencé.

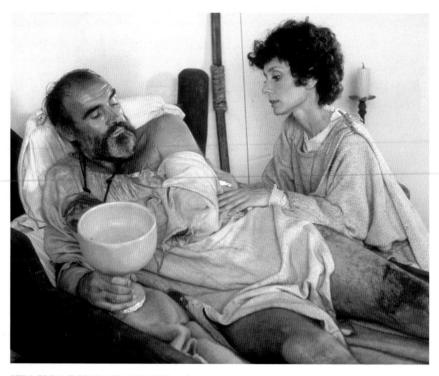

STILL FROM 'ROBIN AND MARIAN' (1976)
In this tale of an old and dying Robin Hood, Connery imbued the role with his own concerns after the death of his father. / Nach dem Tod seines Vaters brachte Connery seine eigenen Belange in diese Geschichte über den alten, im Sterben liegenden Robin Hood ein. / Dans ce conte sur les dernières heures de Robin des Bois, Connery s'inspire des émotions et des questionnements qui furent les siens après la mort de son père.

PORTRAIT FOR 'ROBIN AND MARIAN' (1976)
Connery was happy to film near his new Spanish home, and with quality actors like Audrey Hepburn (as Marian) and Robert Shaw (as the Sheriff of Nottingham). / Connery freute sich, in der Nähe seines neuen Hauses in Spanien und mit talentierten Kollegen wie Audrey Hepburn (als Marian) und Robert Shaw (als Sheriff von Nottingham) drehen zu können. / Connery est heureux de tourner près de sa nouvelle maison, en Espagne, aux côtés d'acteurs de qualité comme Audrey Hepburn (dans le rôle de Marianne) et Robert Shaw (le shérif de Nottingham).

STILL FROM 'THE NEXT MAN' (1976)
In the days before overweening political correctness, Connery plays another Arab character in this thriller, which failed at the box office. / In einer Zeit, bevor der Wahn der „political correctness" grassierte, spielte Connery in diesem Thriller, der beim Publikum floppte, wieder einmal einen Araber. / Bien avant l'ère du politiquement correct, Connery incarne à nouveau un personnage arabe dans ce thriller, qui ne séduit pas le public.

STILL FROM 'A BRIDGE TOO FAR' (1977)
Major General Robert E. Urquhart (Connery) is trying to take the bridge at Arnhem in this massive action pic, based on a true story of World War II. / In diesem aktionsreichen Kriegsepos nach einer wahren Begebenheit aus dem Zweiten Weltkrieg versucht Major General Robert E. Urquhart (Connery), die Brücke von Arnheim einzunehmen. / Le major général Urquhart (Connery) tente de prendre le pont d'Arnhem ; ce film d'action à gros moyens est inspirée d'un épisode réel de la Seconde Guerre mondiale.

STILL FROM 'METEOR' (1979)
Connery plays a scientist trying to deflect an asteroid on a collision course with Earth. The film was a huge flop. / Connery spielt hier einen Wissenschaftler, der versucht, einen Asteroiden von seiner Bahn abzulenken, der sich auf Kollisionskurs mit der Erde befindet. Der Film war ein Flop. / Connery joue un scientifique qui essaie de dévier la trajectoire d'un astéroïde qui doit entrer en collision avec la Terre. Le film est un four.

"Why don't you stick a broom up my ass?
I can sweep the carpet on the way out."
Dr. Paul Bradley, *Meteor* (1979)

„Warum schiebst du mir keinen Besen in den Arsch?
Dann kann ich auf dem Weg nach draußen gleich
noch den Teppich fegen."
Dr. Paul Bradley, *Meteor* (1979)

STILL FROM
'THE FIRST GREAT TRAIN ROBBERY' (1979)
Edward Pierce (Connery) is a master thief in this witty period heist movie. Here he is with accomplice Miriam (Lesley-Anne Down). / In diesem geistreichen Film über einen historischen Eisenbahnraub ist Edward Pierce (Connery) der Meisterdieb – hier im Bild mit seiner Komplizin Miriam (Lesley-Anne Down). / Edward Pierce (Connery) est un voleur chevronné dans ce film d'époque plein d'esprit. Ici accompagné de sa complice, Miriam (Lesley-Anne Down).

« Pourquoi vous ne me carrez pas un balais dans le
derrière ? Je pourrais balayer le tapis en sortant. »
Dr. Paul Bradley, *Meteor* (1979)

STILLS FROM 'CUBA' (1979)

Robert Dapes, a former major in the British army, is hired to teach Batista's troops counterinsurgency measures. Although Connery liked working with director Richard Lester and costar Brooke Adams, they started work with an unfinished script and had numerous technical problems. / Der ehemalige britische Armeemajor Robert Dapes wird vom kubanischen Diktator Batista angeheuert, um dessen Truppen in der Niederschlagung von Aufständen auszubilden. Obwohl Connery gerne mit Regisseur Richard Lester und seiner Kollegin Brooke Adams zusammenarbeitete, begannen die Dreharbeiten, bevor das Drehbuch fertig geschrieben war, und es gab zahlreiche technische Probleme. / Robert Dapes, ancien major de l'armée britannique, est engagé pour enseigner aux troupes de Batista ses méthodes de répression de l'insurrection. Connery apprécia sa collaboration avec le réalisateur

Richard Lester et sa partenaire Brooke Adams, malgré de nombreux problèmes techniques et le fait qu'ils aient commencé à travailler avant que le scénario ne soit achevé.

PAGES 126/127
STILL FROM 'TIME BANDITS' (1981)

Michael Palin and Terry Gilliam named Connery in the script, but they never dreamed that he would agree to play King Agamemnon (right). / Michael Palin und Terry Gilliam erwähnten Connery in ihrem Drehbuch, hätten aber nie zu träumen gewagt, dass dieser tatsächlich die Rolle des Königs Agamemnon (rechts) annehmen würde. / Michael Palin et Terry Gilliam avaient pensé à Connery pendant l'écriture du scénario, mais ils n'auraient jamais pensé qu'il accepterait d'incarner le roi Agamemnon (à droite).

STILLS FROM 'OUTLAND' (1981)
O'Niel (Connery) is the police marshall of a cramped
mining colony in outer space. / O'Niel (Connery)
ist der Polizeimarschall einer dicht besiedelten Berg-
werkskolonie im Weltall. / O'Niel (Connery) est le
chef de la police d'une colonie minière perdue dans
l'espace.

STILL FROM 'OUTLAND' (1981)
When he investigates drug smuggling and murder, O'Niel finds that none of the miners will help him. / Als er Fällen von Drogenschmuggel und Mord auf die Spur kommt, stellt O'Niel fest, dass ihm keiner der Bergarbeiter helfen wird. / Alors qu'il enquête sur une affaire de drogue et de meurtre, O'Niel découvre qu'aucun des mineurs ne l'aidera.

STILL FROM 'OUTLAND' (1981)
Connery believed in the picture, was involved in every aspect of the production, and promoted it. / Connery glaubte an diesen Film, war an allen Aspekten der Produktion beteiligt und warb für ihn. / Connery croit en ce film : il s'investit dans chaque étape de la production et en assure ensuite la promotion.

"In other words you don't do anything bad, you just don't do anything good, do you?"
O'Niel, *Outland* (1981)

„Mit anderen Worten: Du tust nichts Schlimmes, du tust nur einfach nichts Gutes, stimmt's?"
O'Niel, *Outland* (1981)

« Autrement dit, vous ne faites rien de mal, mais vous ne faites rien de bien non plus, c'est ça ? »
O'Niel, *Outland* (1981)

STILL FROM 'WRONG IS RIGHT' (1982)
Patrick Hale (Connery) is a cynical, controversial documentary filmmaker in director Richard Brooks's prescient black comedy about the media, terrorism, and government agencies. / In dieser weitsichtigen schwarzen Komödie des Regisseurs Richard Brooks über Medien, Terrorismus und Behörden ist Patrick Hale (Connery) ein zynischer und umstrittener Dokumentarfilmer. / Patrick Hale (Connery) est un documentariste cynique et controversé dans cette comédie noire prémonitoire de Richard Brooks sur les médias, le terrorisme et les agences gouvernementales.

"I never disliked Bond, as some have thought. Creating a character like that does take a certain craft. It's simply natural to seek other roles."
Sean Connery

„Ich hatte nie eine Abneigung gegen Bond, wie manche dachten. Man benötigt schon ein gewisses Geschick, um eine Figur wie diese zu erschaffen. Es ist ganz natürlich, dass man sich andere Rollen sucht."
Sean Connery

« Je n'ai jamais eu d'aversion pour Bond, comme certains l'ont cru. Il faut un certain art pour créer un personnage comme lui. Il est simplement naturel de chercher d'autres rôles. »
Sean Connery

STILL FROM 'WRONG IS RIGHT' (1982)

As was now normal for Connery, he redrafted his character's dialogue and made notes on the script. Connery now had approval on every aspect of the film productions he appeared in. / Für Connery gehörte es inzwischen zur Normalität, dass er den Text seiner Figuren umschrieb und das Drehbuch mit Anmerkungen versah. Sämtliche Aspekte der Produktionen, in denen er mitwirkte, mussten von ihm abgesegnet werden. / Comme il en a maintenant pris l'habitude, Connery réécrit en partie son texte et annote le scénario. Il jouit désormais d'un droit de regard et d'ajustement total sur les films auxquels il participe.

PAGES 134/135

STILL FROM 'FIVE DAYS ONE SUMMER' (1982)

Connery underwent mountaineering training for the arduous shooting of Fred Zinnemann's film in the Swiss Alps. / Für die anstrengenden Dreharbeiten in den Schweizer Alpen unter der Regie von Fred Zinnemann absolvierte Connery eine Bergsteigerausbildung. / Connery doit apprendre l'alpinisme pour le tournage difficile du film de Fred Zinnemann dans les Alpes suisses.

STILL FROM 'NEVER SAY NEVER AGAIN' (1983)
Connery took a $5 million paycheck to reprise his role
as James Bond in a remake of *Thunderball*. Here he
meets femme fatale Fatima Blush (Barbara Carrera). /
Für eine Gage von fünf Millionen US-Dollar schlüpfte
Connery in diesem Remake von *Feuerball* noch einmal
in die Rolle des James Bond. Hier lernt er die Femme
fatale Fatima Blush (Barbara Carrera) kennen. /
Connery empoche un cachet de 5 millions de dollars
pour revêtir une fois encore le costume de James
Bond dans un remake d'*Opération Tonnerre*.
Il y croise la route de la femme fatale Fatima Blush
(Barbara Carrera).

STILL FROM 'NEVER SAY NEVER AGAIN' (1983)
Bond tangos with Domino (Kim Basinger). / Bond tanzt
Tango mit Domino (Kim Basinger). / Bond danse le
tango avec Domino (Kim Basinger).

PAGES 138/139
STILL FROM 'NEVER SAY NEVER AGAIN' (1983)
Connery controlled the set because he knew the
character better than anybody else. / Connery hatte
die Dreharbeiten im Griff, denn er kannte die Figur
besser als jeder andere. / Connery domine le tournage,
parce qu'il connaît le personnage mieux que quiconque.

STILL FROM 'NEVER SAY NEVER AGAIN' (1983)
Even though Bond is obviously older in the film, he is
still an action man. / Obwohl Bond in diesem Film
sichtlich gealtert erschien, war er noch immer ein Mann
der Tat. / Bond a certes pris de l'âge, mais il reste un
homme d'action.

STILL FROM 'NEVER SAY NEVER AGAIN' (1983)
Ever the professional, Connery did all the stunts he was
able to. / Als Vollprofi drehte Connery sämtliche Stunts
selbst, soweit es möglich war. / Toujours professionnel,
Connery tient à réaliser lui-même autant de cascades
que possible.

STILL FROM 'SWORD OF THE VALIANT: THE LEGEND OF SIR GAWAIN AND THE GREEN KNIGHT' (1984)
This languid retelling of the Arthurian legend only sparkles when Connery is on screen. / Der einzige Lichtblick in dieser trägen Nacherzählung der Artus-Legende war Connery. / Cette reconstitution alanguie de la légende arthurienne ne brille que par la présence de Connery à l'écran.

STILL FROM 'HIGHLANDER' (1986)
Juan Sanchez Villa-Lobos Ramirez (Connery) trains fellow immortal Connor MacLeod (Christopher Lambert) in this entertaining fantasy romp. / Juan Sánchez Villa-Lobos Ramírez (Connery) trainiert in diesem unterhaltsamen Fantasy-Spektakel seinen ebenfalls unsterblichen Kollegen Connor MacLeod (Christopher Lambert). / Juan Sanchez Villa-Lobos Ramirez (Connery) forme le jeune immortel Connor MacLeod (Christophe Lambert) dans cette épopée fantastique fort divertissante.

STILL FROM 'HIGHLANDER' (1986)
Connery enjoyed working in the Scottish Highlands, being a tour guide for Lambert, and spending all his spare time on the golf course. / Connery machte es Spaß, im schottischen Hochland zu drehen, Fremden-führer für Lambert zu spielen und seine freie Zeit auf dem Golfplatz zu verbringen. / Connery prend un grand plaisir à tourner dans les Highlands écossais : il fait visiter la région à Lambert et passe tout son temps libre sur les parcours de golf.

STILL FROM 'HIGHLANDER' (1986)
Ramirez is tragically killed by the evil Kurgan (Clancy Brown). / Ramírez wird von dem bösen Kurgan (Clancy Brown) auf tragische Weise umgebracht. / Ramirez est tragiquement assassiné par le Kurgan (Clancy Brown).

STILLS FROM 'THE NAME OF THE ROSE' (1986)

Brother William of Baskerville investigates a puzzling series of murders in this film version of Umberto Eco's novel. The film encapsulated everything Connery loves about movies, with quality characters and a quality script brought to life by a professional cast and crew in subzero conditions. / In dieser Verfilmung des Romans von Umberto Eco untersucht Bruder William von Baskerville eine Reihe rätselhafter Morde in einem Kloster. Der Film hatte alles, was Connery an seinem Beruf mag: gut gezeichnete Figuren, die bei Temperaturen unter dem Gefrierpunkt von Profis vor und hinter der Kamera nach einem gut geschriebenen Drehbuch zum Leben erweckt wurden. / Le frère William de Baskerville enquête sur une mystérieuse série de meurtres dans ce film tiré du roman d'Umberto Eco. Celui-ci rassemble tout ce que Connery aime dans le cinéma : personnages bien construits, scénario de qualité, vrais professionnels devant et derrière la caméra, froid polaire sur le lieu de tournage...

PAGES 148/149
STILL FROM 'THE NAME OF THE ROSE' (1986)

Many of Connery's films now followed a standard dynamic. If there was no leading lady on his arm, then he played master to a student—in this case Adso (Christian Slater). / Viele von Connerys Filmen folgten nun einer bestimmten Dynamik: Wenn er keine Dame an seiner Seite hatte, dann spielte er den Lehrmeister eines Schülers – in diesem Fall Adso (Christian Slater). / La plupart des films de Connery suivent dès lors une dynamique similaire. S'il n'a pas une beauté à son bras, il joue un maître formant un élève – ici, Adso (Christian Slater).

"You just fulfilled the first rule of law enforcement: Make sure when your shift is over you go home alive. Here endeth the lesson."
Jim Malone, *The Untouchables* (1987)

„Sie haben soeben die erste Regel der Polizeiarbeit beherzigt: Sorge dafür, dass du am Ende deiner Schicht lebendig nach Hause gehst. Ende der Lektion."
Jim Malone, *The Untouchables: Die Unbestechlichen* (1987)

« Vous venez de mettre en pratique la première règle du maintien de l'ordre : s'assurer qu'à la fin du service vous rentrez chez vous en vie. Ici s'achève la leçon. »
Jim Malone, *Les Incorruptibles* (1987)

STILL FROM 'THE UNTOUCHABLES' (1987)
Jim Malone (Connery) mentors G-man Eliot Ness (Kevin Costner): "You want to get Capone? Here's how you get him: They pull a knife, you pull a gun. He sends one of yours to the hospital, you send one of his to the morgue. That's the Chicago way!" / Jim Malone (Connery) gibt "G-Man" Eliot Ness (Kevin Costner) einen Rat: „Sie wollen Capone? Ich sag Ihnen, wie Sie ihn kriegen! Er kommt mit 'nem Messer – Sie mit 'ner Kanone. Er schickt einen von euch ins Krankenhaus – Sie einen von denen ins Leichenhaus. So wird das in Chicago gemacht!" / Jim Malone (Connery) est le mentor d'Eliot Ness (Kevin Costner) : « Vous voulez attraper Capone ? Voilà comment vous l'aurez : ils sortent un couteau, vous sortez un flingue. Il envoie un des vôtres à l'hôpital, vous envoyez un des leurs à la morgue. C'est comme ça que ça se passe, à Chicago ! »

STILL FROM 'THE UNTOUCHABLES' (1987)
Connery won an Oscar for his performance, here with Agent Oscar Wallace (Charles Martin Smith), Eliot Ness, and Agent George Stone (Andy Garcia). / Connery wurde für seine Leistung in diesem Film mit einem „Oscar" ausgezeichnet. Hier ist er als Malone mit Eliot Ness und den Agenten Oscar Wallace (Charles Martin Smith, ganz links) und George Stone (Andy Garcia, ganz rechts) zu sehen. / Connery remporte un oscar pour sa prestation, ici avec l'agent Oscar Wallace (Charles Martin Smith), Eliot Ness et l'agent George Stone (Andy Garcia).

PAGES 152/153
STILL FROM 'THE PRESIDIO' (1988)
To capitalize on his Oscar win, Connery embarked on a number of roles. Back in uniform, much older but still tough as nails, Caldwell (Connery) investigates a murder. / Connery nahm eine Reihe von Rollen an, um aus seinem „Oscar" Kapital zu schlagen. Wieder in Uniform, deutlich älter, aber immer noch hart im Nehmen, untersucht er als Caldwell einen Mord. / Pour tirer parti de son oscar, Connery enchaîne les rôles. Plus âgé mais l'esprit toujours acéré, Caldwell (Connery) enquête sur un meurtre.

**STILL FROM 'INDIANA JONES
AND THE LAST CRUSADE' (1989)**
Indiana's father was first envisioned as a weak
professor type, but once Connery was on board
the whole dynamic changed and Indiana had to defer
to his father. / Indianas Vater war ursprünglich als
schwächlicher Gelehrtentyp konzipiert worden, doch
als Connery die Rolle übernahm, änderte sich die
gesamte Dynamik, und Indiana musste sich seinem
Vater unterordnen. / Le père d'Indiana apparaît
d'abord comme un professeur d'université plutôt
rouillé, mais dès que Connery entre en scène, la
dynamique change et Indiana doit s'incliner devant lui.

*"Those people are trying to kill us. This is a new
experience for me."*
Professor Henry Jones, *Indiana Jones and the Last
Crusade* (1989)

*„Diese Leute versuchen, uns umzubringen. Das ist
eine neue Erfahrung für mich."*
Professor Henry Jones, *Indiana Jones und der letzte
Kreuzzug* (1989)

*« Ces gens essaient de nous tuer. C'est une
expérience nouvelle pour moi. »*
Professeur Henry Jones, *Indiana Jones et la dernière
croisade* (1989)

**STILL FROM 'INDIANA JONES
AND THE LAST CRUSADE' (1989)**
Tom Stoppard's uncredited rewrite of Connery's part
made the interplay between Indiana (Harrison Ford)
and Professor Jones the highlight of the film. / Dank
Tom Stoppard, der Connerys Dialogteile umschrieb,
ohne dass er dafür namentlich erwähnt wurde, gedieh
das Wechselspiel zwischen Indiana (Harrison Ford) und
seinem Vater zu einem der Glanzlichter des Films. /
Tom Stoppard (non crédité) réécrit si bien le rôle de
Connery que l'interaction entre Indiana (Harrison Ford)
et le professeur Jones devient le principal intérêt
du film.

STILL FROM 'FAMILY BUSINESS' (1989)
Sidney Lumet's hard-edged crime comedy has career criminal Jessie McMullen (Connery) return to wreak havoc with his grandson Adam (Matthew Broderick) and son Vito (Dustin Hoffman). / In Sidney Lumets knallharter Kriminalkomödie kehrt der Berufsverbrecher Jessie McMullen (Connery) noch einmal zurück, um das Leben seines Enkels Adam (Matthew Broderick) und seines Sohns Vito (Dustin Hoffman) auf den Kopf zu stellen. / Dans cette comédie criminelle acide, le malfrat professionnel Jessie McMullen (Connery) fait des ravages avec son petit-fils Adam (Matthew Broderick) et son fils Vito (Dustin Hoffman).

"You're afraid of our fleet. Well, you should be. Personally, I give us one chance in three. More tea, anyone?"
Captain Marko Ramius, *The Hunt for Red October* (1990)

**STILL FROM
'THE HUNT FOR RED OCTOBER' (1990)**
Connery returned after suffering from throat problems
to play defecting Soviet submarine captain Marko
Ramius, here with Jack Ryan (Alec Baldwin). /
Nach einer Halskrankheit kehrte Connery in der
Rolle des sowjetischen U-Boot-Kapitäns Marko Ramius
auf die Leinwand zurück, der hier mit Jack Ryan
(Alec Baldwin) zu sehen ist. / Après avoir eu des
problèmes à la gorge, Connery revient sur les plateaux
pour jouer le capitaine de sous-marin Marko Ramius,
ici avec Jack Ryan (Alec Baldwin).

„*Sie fürchten sich vor unserer Flotte. Nun,
das sollten Sie auch. Persönlich gebe ich uns
eine Chance von eins zu drei. Möchte noch
jemand Tee?*"
Kapitän Marko Ramius, *Jagd auf Roter Oktober* (1990)

« *Vous avez peur de notre flotte. Eh bien, vous
devriez. Personnellement, je nous donne une
chance sur trois. Quelqu'un reveut du thé ?* »
Capitaine Marko Ramius, *À la poursuite d'Octobre
Rouge* (1990)

"I prefer Russia. It's as corrupt as America, but there's less bullshit."
Bartholomew "Barley" Scott Blair, *The Russia House* (1990)

„Ich ziehe Russland vor. Es ist ebenso korrupt wie Amerika, aber es gibt weniger Scheiß."
Bartholomew „Barley" Scott Blair, *Das Russland-Haus* (1990)

« Je préfère la Russie. Elle est aussi corrompue que l'Amérique, mais il y a moins de conneries. »
Bartholomew « Barley » Scott Blair, *La Maison Russie* (1990)

STILL FROM 'THE RUSSIA HOUSE' (1990)
Publisher "Barley" Scott Blair (Connery) falls for Katya (Michelle Pfeiffer) while spying in Russia. / Der Verleger „Barley" Scott Blair (Connery) verliebt sich in Katya (Michelle Pfeiffer), während er in Russland spioniert. / L'éditeur « Barley » Scott Blair (Connery) tombe sous le charme de Katya (Michelle Pfeiffer) alors qu'il fait l'espion en Russie.

**STILL FROM 'HIGHLANDER II:
THE QUICKENING' (1991)**
Connery's character was "resurrected" to ensure fiscal success for this sequel. Connery donated his fee to charity. / Es kann doch einen zweiten (Teil) geben: Connerys Figur feierte „Wiederauferstehung", um den finanziellen Erfolg dieser Fortsetzung abzusichern. Connery spendete seine Gage für wohltätige Zwecke. / Le personnage de Connery est « ramené à la vie » pour garantir le succès financier de cette suite. Connery reverse son cachet à des œuvres de charité.

**STILL FROM 'ROBIN HOOD:
PRINCE OF THIEVES' (1991)**
After befriending Kevin Costner, Connery agreed to make a cameo appearance as King Richard, and again gave his fee to his Scottish charity. / Nachdem er sich mit Kevin Costner angefreundet hatte, ließ sich Connery von ihm zu einem Cameo-Auftritt als König Richard überreden und spendete seine Gage erneut einer schottischen Wohltätigkeitsorganisation. / Parce qu'il s'est lié d'amitié avec Kevin Costner, Connery accepte d'apparaître dans le rôle du roi Richard et fait une fois encore don de son cachet à une association caritative écossaise.

STILL FROM 'MEDICINE MAN' (1992)
Connery withstood heat, humidity, parasites, and dangerous stunts to make this message film about the disappearing rain forests. Here he is with his leading lady, Lorraine Bracco. / Connery setzte sich Hitze, Schwüle, Parasiten und gefährlichen Stunts aus, um diesen mahnenden Film über das Verschwinden des Regenwalds zu drehen. Hier ist er mit seiner Kollegin Lorraine Bracco zu sehen. / Connery n'hésite pas à affronter chaleur, humidité, parasites et cascades dangereuses pour participer à ce film engagé sur la disparition des forêts tropicales. Le voici avec sa partenaire à l'écran, Lorraine Bracco.

STILL FROM 'RISING SUN' (1993)
Lt. Webster Smith (Wesley Snipes) needs the help of Japanese expert John Connor (Connery) to navigate a murder investigation at a Japanese corporation. / Lieutenant Webster Smith (Wesley Snipes) benötigt die Hilfe des Japanexperten John Connor (Connery), um einen Mord in einem japanischen Unternehmen aufzuklären. / Le lieutenant Webster Smith (Wesley Snipes) sollicite l'aide de l'expert du Japon John Connor (Connery) pour mener l'enquête sur un meurtre commis dans une firme japonaise.

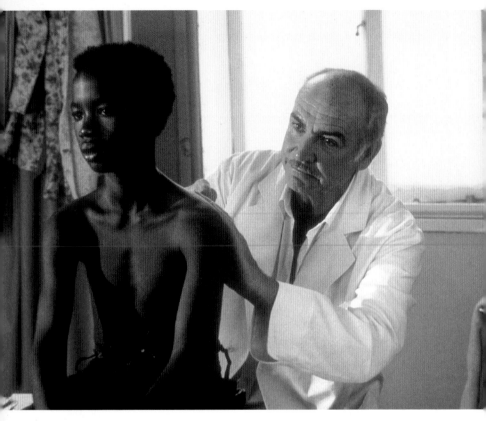

STILL FROM 'A GOOD MAN IN AFRICA' (1994)
Connery plays a selfless physician in this comedy
based on William Boyd's novel. / Connery spielt in
dieser Komödie nach dem Roman von William Boyd
einen selbstlosen Arzt. / Connery joue un médecin
altruiste dans cette comédie basée sur un roman de
William Boyd.

"If that's a confession then my ass is a banjo."
Paul Armstrong, *Just Cause* (1995)

*„Wenn das ein Geständnis sein soll, dann ist mein
Arsch ein Banjo."*
Paul Armstrong, *Im Sumpf des Verbrechens* (1995)

*« Si ça c'est une confession, alors mon cul est
un banjo. »*
Paul Armstrong, *Juste cause* (1995)

STILL FROM 'JUST CAUSE' (1995)
Connery was again executive producer on this socially
conscious drama about Southern injustice and racism.
Here Paul Armstrong (Connery) confronts Blair Sullivan
(Ed Harris). / In diesem gesellschaftskritischen Drama
über Ungerechtigkeit und Rassismus in den Südstaaten
der USA war Connery erneut auch ausführender
Produzent. Hier stellt Paul Armstrong (Connery) Blair
Sullivan (Ed Harris) zur Rede. / Connery coiffe une fois
de plus la casquette de producteur exécutif pour ce
drame social sur l'injustice et le racisme qui règne dans
le Sud américain. Ici, Paul Armstrong (Connery) affronte
Blair Sullivan (Ed Harris).

*"I take the good with the bad, together. I can't love
people in slices."*
King Arthur, *First Knight* (1995)

*„Ich nehme das Gute mit dem Bösen, zusammen.
Ich kann Menschen nicht scheibenweise lieben."*
King Arthur, *Der 1. Ritter* (1995)

*« Je prends le bon et le mauvais ensemble. Je ne
peux pas aimer les gens par tranches. »*
Le roi Arthur, *Lancelot* (1995)

STILL FROM 'DRAGONHEART' (1996)
Draco's expressions were culled from Connery's back catalog, so the face was authentic to his voice-over. / Die Mimik des Drachen Draco basierte auf alten Bildern und Filmausschnitten mit Connery, sodass das Gesicht in der Originalfassung perfekt zur Stimme passte. / Les expressions de Draco ont été puisées dans le vaste éventail de Connery pour que la voix semble plus authentique.

STILL FROM 'FIRST KNIGHT' (1995)
Connery played King Arthur in this uninteresting telling of the tragic romance between Arthur, Guinevere (Julia Ormond), and Lancelot. / In dieser harmlosen Verfilmung der tragischen Romanze zwischen Artus, Guinevere (Julia Ormond) und Lancelot spielt Connery den sagenhaften König. / Connery joue le roi Arthur dans ce récit inintéressant de la tragique histoire entre le roi, sa femme Guenièvre (Julia Ormond) et Lancelot (Richard Gere).

STILL FROM 'THE ROCK' (1996)
John Patrick Mason (Connery), a clandestine British agent long imprisoned in the United States, reluctantly helps Dr. Stanley Goodspeed (Nicolas Cage) break into Alcatraz to disarm some biological weapons. / John Patrick Mason (Connery), ein britischer Geheimagent, der lange Zeit in den USA im Gefängnis saß, hilft Dr. Stanley Goodspeed (Nicolas Cage) widerwillig, in das ehemalige Gefängnis von Alcatraz einzubrechen, um dort biologische Waffen zu vernichten. / John Patrick Mason (Connery), un agent secret britannique longtemps détenu aux États-Unis, aide à contrecœur Stanley Goodspeed (Nicolas Cage) à s'introduire dans la prison d'Alcatraz pour détruire des armes biologiques.

STILL FROM 'THE ROCK' (1996)
There was some tough stunt work for a 65-year-old, and clashes with director Michael Bay, but Connery stole the film. / Für einen 65-Jährigen waren einige der Stunts ziemlich hart, und Connery lag sich zeitweise mit Regisseur Michael Bay in den Haaren, aber letztendlich drückte der Schotte dem Film seinen Stempel auf. / Certaines cascades sont rudes pour un homme de 65 ans et ses rapports avec le réalisateur Michael Bay sont houleux, mais Connery illumine le film.

STILL FROM 'THE AVENGERS' (1998)
The successful 1960s TV show ran parallel to the
Connery Bond movies. / Die erfolgreiche Fernsehserie
lief in den 1960er-Jahren parallel zu Connerys Bond-
Filmen. / Cette série télévisée remporte un grand
succès dans les années 1960, au même moment où
Connery incarne James Bond au grand écran.

STILL FROM 'PLAYING BY HEART' (1998)
In this sensitive relationship movie, Hannah (Gena
Rowlands) asks Paul (Connery) about an old affair. /
In diesem gefühlvollen Beziehungsfilm befragt Hannah
(Gena Rowlands) Paul (Connery) zu einer alten Affäre. /
Film sensible et dense où Hannah (Gena Rowlands)
interroge Paul (Connery) sur une liaison passée.

STILL FROM 'ENTRAPMENT' (1999)
Master thief Robert MacDougal (Connery) is hounded
by investigator Virginia Baker (Catherine Zeta-Jones)
in this sexy, fun heist thriller. / Meisterdieb Robert
MacDougal (Connery) wird in diesem witzig-erotischen
Diebstahlthriller von der Versicherungssachverstän-
digen Virginia Baker (Catherine Zeta-Jones) gejagt. /
L'as du cambriolage Robert MacDougal (Connery)
est traqué par l'enquêteuse Virginia Baker (Catherine
Zeta-Jones) dans ce thriller enlevé et sexy.

STILL FROM 'FINDING FORRESTER' (2000)
Jamal (Rob Brown) is tutored by reclusive author
William Forrester (Connery) in a film directed by Gus
Van Sant. / In diesem Film von Gus Van Sant erhält
Jamal (Rob Brown) Nachhilfe von dem zurückgezogen
lebenden Schriftsteller William Forrester (Connery). /
L'auteur solitaire William Forrester (Connery) prend
Jamal (Rob Brown) sous son aile dans ce film réalisé
par Gus Van Sant.

**STILL FROM 'THE LEAGUE OF
EXTRAORDINARY GENTLEMEN' (2003)**
In 1899, Allan Quatermain (Connery) leads a team of
adventurers against the war-mongering "Fantom", but
finds time to mentor Tom Sawyer (Shane West). /
Im Jahre 1899 führt Allan Quatermain (Connery) ein
Team von Abenteurern im Kampf gegen das kriegs-
treiberische „Phantom", wobei ihm noch genügend Zeit
bleibt, Tom Sawyer (Shane West) Schießunterricht zu
geben. / En 1899, Allan Quatermain (Connery) conduit
une équipe d'aventuriers sur les traces du « Fantôme »,
et trouve le temps de former le jeune Tom Sawyer
(Shane West).

*"Very American. Fire enough bullets and hope
to hit the target."*
Allan Quatermain, *The League of Extraordinary
Gentlemen* (2003)

*„Sehr amerikanisch. Genügend Kugeln verballern
und hoffen, dass man dabei das Ziel trifft."*
Allan Quatermain, *Die Liga der außergewöhnlichen
Gentlemen* (2003)

*« Très américain. Tirer des tonnes de munitions
en espérant atteindre la cible. »*
Allan Quatermain, *La Ligue des gentlemen
extraordinaires* (2003)

PAGES 176/177

STILL FROM 'THE LEAGUE OF EXTRAORDINARY GENTLEMEN' (2003)
Quatermain with Captain Nemo, Dorian Gray, and The Invisible Man. / Quatermain mit Kapitän Nemo, Dorian Gray und dem Unsichtbaren. / Quatermain aux côtés du capitaine Nemo, de Dorian Gray et de l'Homme invisible.

PAGE 178

PORTRAIT FOR 'HIGHLANDER' (1986)

STILL FROM 'THE LEAGUE OF EXTRAORDINARY GENTLEMEN' (2003)
After turning down *The Matrix* and *The Lord of the Rings*, Connery wanted to be part of a successful series, but he was so dismayed by the way the production was made and its lack of fiscal success that he retired from filmmaking. / Nachdem er Rollen in *Matrix* und *Herr der Ringe* abgelehnt hatte, wollte Connery endlich auch in einer erfolgreichen Filmreihe mitspielen, doch er war von dieser Produktion und ihrem finanziellen Misserfolg so enttäuscht, dass er sich anschließend aus dem Filmgeschäft zurückzog. / Après avoir refusé *Matrix* et *Le Seigneur des anneaux*, Connery a envie de participer à une saga à succès, mais il est si déçu par la façon dont la production s'organise et dont l'argent circule qu'il annonce son départ en retraite.

3

CHRONOLOGY

CHRONOLOGIE

CHRONOLOGIE

CHRONOLOGY

25 August 1930 Thomas Sean Connery is born in the Fountainbridge district of Edinburgh to Joseph Connery and Euphamia C. "Effie" MacLean.

1947 Joins the Royal Navy at 16. Mustered out after three years because of an ulcer.

1950 Works variously as a truck driver, bricklayer, lifeguard, polisher of brass fittings on coffins, music-hall bouncer, and—after he takes up body-building—figure model.

1953 In London, places third in the Mr. Universe Junior Class competition. In June, auditions for a touring company of *South Pacific*.

1954 Is an extra in the Errol Flynn musical *Lilacs in the Spring*.

1957 Meets first wife, Diane Cilento, when they are cast as star-crossed lovers in *Anna Christie*. (They marry in 1962 and divorce in 1973.) Signs a contract with 20th Century Fox.

1959 Concentrates on stage work after Cilento contracts tuberculosis.

1961 Appears in *Anna Karenina* for the BBC and *Macbeth* for Canadian television.

1962 Upon the advice of director Terence Young, producers Albert R. "Cubby" Broccoli and Harry Saltzman sign Connery to portray James Bond in five pictures, beginning with *Dr. No*.

1964 Earns his first seven-figure salary for *Woman of Straw*.

1970 Directs a play with Diane Cilento. Meets his second wife, Micheline Roquebrune, on a Moroccan golf course; they marry in 1975.

1971 Uses his $1.25 million salary from *Diamonds Are Forever* to found the Scottish International Education Trust for underprivileged children. Also donates his earnings from *The Anderson Tapes*.

1972 Is de facto producer of *The Offence* under a two-picture deal with United Artists.

1973 Unable to get additional financing from United Artists for such projects as *Macbeth* and a biography of Sir Richard Burton, returns to being an actor for hire.

1983 Paid $5 million to return to Bond on a project not owned by United Artists, *Never Say Never Again*. Has his wrist broken by his martial-arts instructor, Steven Seagal.

1984 Sues Albert R. "Cubby" Broccoli for $225 million he is purportedly owed from Bond profit participation.

1987 Wins Academy Award (best supporting actor) for *The Untouchables*.

1990 Wins British Academy of Film and Television Arts Lifetime Achievement Award.

1991 Awarded the Freedom of the City of Edinburgh for his work on Scottish causes. Also receives the French Légion d'honneur.

5 July 2000 Wearing the tartan kilt of the MacLean of Duart clan, knighted by Queen Elizabeth II.

2002 Establishes his official website: www.seanconnery.com.

2005 Announces his retirement from movie acting.

2006 Wins American Film Institute Life Achievement Award.

**STILL FROM
'FROM RUSSIA WITH LOVE' (1963)**

CHRONOLOGIE

25. August 1930 Thomas Sean Connery wird in Edinburgh, im Bezirk Fountainbridge, als Sohn von Joseph Connery und Euphamia C. „Effie" MacLean geboren.

1947 Mit 16 tritt er in die königliche Marine ein und wird nach drei Jahren aufgrund eines Magengeschwürs ausgemustert.

1950 Er arbeitet als Lkw-Fahrer, Maurer, Rettungsschwimmer und Türsteher, poliert Messingbeschläge an Särgen und steht schließlich, nachdem er mit dem Bodybuilding begonnen hat, für Kunststudenten Modell.

1953 In London belegt er den dritten Platz in der Juniorenklasse des Mister-Universum-Wettbewerbs. Im Juni spricht er bei einer Wanderbühne vor, die mit dem Musical *South Pacific* durch die Lande zieht.

1954 Er spielt eine Statistenrolle in dem Errol-Flynn-Musical *Lilacs in the Spring*.

1957 Er trifft seine spätere erste Ehefrau, Diane Cilento, als die beiden in *Anna Christie* ein Paar spielen, dessen Liebe unter einem schlechten Stern steht. (Die beiden heiraten 1962 und werden 1973 geschieden.) Er wird von 20th Century Fox unter Vertrag genommen.

1959 Nachdem Cilento an Tuberkulose erkrankt, konzentriert er sich auf das Theater.

1961 Er tritt für die BBC in *Anna Karenina* und für das kanadische Fernsehen in *Macbeth* auf.

1962 Auf Anraten des Regisseurs Terence Young verpflichten die Produzenten Albert R. „Cubby" Broccoli und Harry Saltzman Connery, in fünf Filmen James Bond darzustellen, angefangen mit *James Bond 007 jagt Dr. No*.

1964 Er verdient seine erste siebenstellige Gage für *Die Strohpuppe*.

1970 Er inszeniert ein Theaterstück mit Diane Cilento. Er lernt auf einem marokkanischen Golfplatz seine spätere zweite Ehefrau, Micheline Roquebrune, kennen, die er 1975 heiratet.

STILL FROM 'CUBA' (1979)

1971 Er verwendet seine Gage in Höhe von 1,25 Millionen US-Dollar, die er für *Diamantenfieber* erhält, um den Scottish International Education Trust für unterprivilegierte Kinder zu gründen. Er stiftet auch die Gage, die er für *Der Anderson-Clan* erhält.

1972 Im Rahmen eines Vertrags mit United Artists über zwei Filme wird er de facto zum Produzenten von *Sein Leben in meiner Gewalt*.

1973 Weil er nicht in der Lage ist, zusätzliche finanzielle Mittel von United Artists für Projekte wie *Macbeth* und eine Biografie von Sir Richard Burton zu bekommen, kehrt er zur reinen Schauspielerei zurück.

1983 Er erhält 5 Millionen US-Dollar, um Bond noch einmal in der Verfilmung eines Buches zu spielen, dessen Rechte United Artists nicht besitzt: *Sag niemals nie*. Steven Seagal, der ihn in Kampfkunst unterrichtet, bricht ihm versehentlich das Handgelenk.

1984 Er verklagt Albert R. „Cubby" Broccoli auf 225 Millionen US-Dollar, die dieser ihm angeblich noch als Gewinnbeteiligung aus den Bond-Filmen schuldet.

1987 Er erhält einen Academy Award (als bester Darsteller in einer Nebenrolle) für *The Untouchables: Die Unbestechlichen*.

1990 Er erhält den Lifetime Achievement Award der British Academy of Film and Television Arts.

1991 Für seinen Einsatz für schottische Angelegenheiten erhält er die Auszeichnung „Freedom of the City of Edinburgh". Außerdem wird er in die französische Ehrenlegion aufgenommen.

5. Juli 2000 Im Tartan-Kilt des Clans der MacLean of Duart wird Connery von Königin Elisabeth II. zum Ritter geschlagen.

2002 Seine offizielle Website geht online: www.seanconnery.com.

Juli 2005 Er kündigt seinen Rückzug aus der Schauspielerei an.

2006 Er erhält den Life Achievement Award des American Film Institute.

CHRONOLOGIE

25 août 1930 Naissance de Thomas Sean Connery, fils de Joseph Connery et Euphamia C. « Effie » MacLean, dans le quartier de Fountainbridge à Édimbourg.

1947 À l'âge de 16 ans, il s'engage dans la Royal Navy. Il est rapatrié après trois années de service en raison d'un ulcère à l'estomac.

1950 Travaille tour à tour comme chauffeur-livreur, maçon, maître-nageur, polisseur de cercueils, videur de boîtes de nuit, et enfin – après s'être mis au culturisme –, pose comme modèle pour artistes.

1953 À Londres, il arrive troisième du concours de Monsieur Univers, catégorie junior. En juin, il auditionne pour un rôle dans la pièce South Pacific, qui tourne alors en Grande-Bretagne.

1954 Engagé comme figurant dans la comédie musicale Voyage en Birmanie, avec Errol Flynn.

1957 Rencontre sa première épouse, Diane Cilento, lorsqu'ils sont tous deux engagés pour incarner un couple maudit dans Anna Christie. (Ils se marieront en 1962 et divorceront en 1973.) Signe un contrat avec la 20th Century Fox.

1959 Se concentre sur le théâtre lorsque Cilento contracte la tuberculose.

1961 Figure dans une version d'Anna Karénine pour la BBC et dans un Macbeth pour la télévision canadienne.

1962 Sur les conseils du réalisateur Terence Young, les producteurs Broccoli et Saltzman l'engagent pour jouer James Bond dans cinq films ; le premier est James Bond 007 contre Dr. No.

1964 Empoche son premier cachet à sept chiffres pour La Femme de paille.

1970 Met en scène une pièce avec Diane Cilento. Rencontre sa seconde épouse, Micheline Roquebrune, sur un parcours de golf marocain ; ils se marieront en 1975.

1971 Utilise le cachet de 1,25 million de dollars qu'il a touché avec Les diamants sont éternels

pour fonder le Scottish International Education Trust, destiné aux enfants démunis. Il fait également don de son cachet du film Gang Anderson.

1972 Produit de facto The Offence en vertu d'un contrat pour deux films signé avec United Artists.

1973 United Artists refusant d'apporter le financement complémentaire nécessaire pour l'adaptation au grand écran de Macbeth et d'une biographie de Sir Richard Burton, il retourne au métier d'acteur indépendant.

1983 Reçoit 5 millions de dollars pour reprendre le rôle de Bond dans un projet indépendant de United Artists, Jamais plus jamais. Son instructeur d'arts martiaux, Steven Seagal, lui brise le poignet.

1984 Poursuit Albert « Cubby » Broccoli en justice et réclame 225 millions de dollars en guise de participation aux bénéfices générés par la saga des Bond.

1987 Remporte l'oscar du Meilleur second rôle masculin pour sa prestation dans Les Incorruptibles.

1990 Reçoit le prix de la British Academy of Film and Television Arts pour l'ensemble de sa carrière.

1991 Reçoit le Prix Freedom of Edinburgh pour son combat en faveur de la cause écossaise. Est fait chevalier de la Légion d'honneur française.

5 juillet 2000 Arborant le kilt en tartan du clan des MacLean de Duart, il est fait chevalier par la reine Elizabeth II.

2002 Crée son site Internet officiel : www.seanconnery.com.

Juillet 2005 Annonce sa retraite du grand écran.

2006 Remporte le prix de l'American Film Institute pour l'ensemble de sa carrière.

PORTRAIT (SEPTEMBER 1983)

4
FILMOGRAPHY

FILMOGRAFIE

FILMOGRAPHIE

Lilacs in the Spring (fr. *Voyage en Birmanie*, 1954)
Uncredited/ungenannt/non crédité.
Director/Regie/réalisation: Herbert Wilcox.

Time Lock (1957)
Second Welder/2. Schweißer/2ᵉ soudeur.
Director/Regie/réalisation: Gerald Thomas.

**No Road Back (dt. *Die blinde Spinne*,
fr. *Les Criminels de Londres*, 1957)**
Spike. Director/Regie/réalisation: Montgomery Tully.

**Hell Drivers (dt. *Duell am Steuer*, fr. *Train
d'enfer*, 1957)**
Johnny Kates. Director/Regie/réalisation: Cy Endfield.

**Action of the Tiger (dt. *Operation Tiger*,
fr. *Au bord du volcan*, 1957)**
Mike. Director/Regie/réalisation: Terence Young.

**A Night to Remember (dt. *Die letzte Nacht der
Titanic*, fr. *Atlantique, latitude 41°*, 1959)**

Deck Hand/Matrose/un homme sur le pont.
Director/Regie/réalisation: Roy Ward Baker.

**Another Time, Another Place (dt. *Herz ohne
Hoffnung*, fr. *Je pleure mon amour*, 1958)**
Mark Trevor. Director/Regie/réalisation: Lewis Allen.

**Tarzan's Greatest Adventure (dt. *Tarzans
größtes Abenteuer*, fr. *La Plus Grande Aventure
de Tarzan*, 1959)**
O'Bannion. Director/Regie/réalisation: John Guillermin.

**Darby O'Gill and the Little People (dt. *Das
Geheimnis der verwunschenen Höhle*, fr. *Darby
O'Gill et les farfadets*, 1959)**
Michael McBride. Director/Regie/réalisation: Lewis
Allen.

**The Frightened City (dt. *Die Peitsche*,
fr. *L'Enquête mystérieuse*, 1961)**
Paddy Damion. Director/Regie/réalisation:
John Lemont.

On the Fiddle (dt. *Das Schlitzohr*, fr. *Deux des commandos*, 1961)
Pedlar Pascoe. Director/Regie/réalisation: Cyril Frankel.

The Longest Day (dt. *Der längste Tag*, fr. *Le Jour le plus long*, 1962)
Private/Soldat/soldat Flanagan. Director/Regie/réalisation: Ken Annakin.

Dr. No (dt. *James Bond 007 jagt Dr. No*, fr. *James Bond 007 contre Dr. No*, 1962)
James Bond. Director/Regie/réalisation: Terence Young.

From Russia with Love (dt. *Liebesgrüße aus Moskau*, fr. *Bons baisers de Russie*, 1963)
James Bond. Director/Regie/réalisation: Terence Young.

Woman of Straw (dt. *Die Strohpuppe*, fr. *La Femme de paille*, 1964)
Anthony "Toni" Richmond. Director/Regie/réalisation: Basil Dearden.

Marnie (fr. *Pas de printemps pour Marnie*, 1964)
Mark Rutland. Director/Regie/réalisation: Alfred Hitchcock.

Goldfinger (1964)
James Bond. Director/Regie/réalisation: Guy Hamilton.

The Hill (dt. *Ein Haufen toller Hunde*, fr. *La Colline des hommes perdus*, 1965)
Trooper/Soldat/soldat Joe Roberts. Director/Regie/réalisation: Sidney Lumet.

Thunderball (dt. *Feuerball*, fr. *Opération Tonnerre*, 1965)
James Bond. Director/Regie/réalisation: Terence Young.

A Fine Madness (dt. *Simson ist nicht zu schlagen*, fr. *L'Homme à la tête fêlée*, 1966)
Samson Shillitoe. Director/Regie/réalisation: Irvin Kershner.

You Only Live Twice (dt. *Man lebt nur zweimal*, fr. *On ne vit que deux fois*, 1967)
James Bond. Director/Regie/réalisation: Lewis Gilbert.

Shalako (dt. *Man nennt mich Shalako*, 1968)
Moses Zebulon "Shalako" Carlin. Director/Regie/réalisation: Edward Dmytryk.

Krasnaya palatka (eng. *The Red Tent*, dt. *Das rote Zelt*, fr. *La Tente rouge*, 1969)
Roald Amundsen. Director/Regie/réalisation: Mikhail Kalatozov.

The Molly Maguires (dt. *Verflucht bis zum jüngsten Tag*, fr. *Traître sur commande*, 1970)
Jack Kehoe. Director/Regie/réalisation: Martin Ritt.

The Anderson Tapes (dt. *Der Anderson-Clan*, fr. *Le Gang Anderson*, 1971)
John Anderson. Director/Regie/réalisation: Sidney Lumet.

Diamonds Are Forever (dt. *Diamantenfieber*, fr. *Les diamants sont éternels*, 1971)
James Bond. Director/Regie/réalisation: Guy Hamilton.

The Offence (dt. *Sein Leben in meiner Gewalt*, 1973)
Detective Sergeant Johnson [also uncredited producer/sowie ungenannt als Produzent/également producteur, non crédité]. Director/Regie/réalisation: Sidney Lumet.

Zardoz (1974)
Zed. Director/Regie/réalisation: John Boorman.

Murder on the Orient Express (dt. *Mord im Orient-Express*, fr. *Le Crime de l'Orient-Express*, 1974)
Colonel Arbuthnot. Director/Regie/réalisation: Sidney Lumet.

The Terrorists (aka *Ransom*, dt. *Die Uhr läuft ab*, fr. *Un homme voit rouge*, 1975)
Nils Tahlvik. Director/Regie/réalisation: Caspar Wrede.

The Wind and the Lion (dt. *Der Wind und der Löwe*, fr. *Le Lion et le Vent*, 1975)
Mulay Achmed Mohammed el-Raisuli the Magnificent/Al-Raisuli le Magnifique. Director/Regie/réalisation: John Milius.

The Man Who Would Be King (dt. *Der Mann, der König sein wollte*, fr. *L'Homme qui voulut être roi*, 1975)
Daniel Dravot. Director/Regie/réalisation: John Huston.

The Next Man (dt. *Der nächste Mann*, fr. alias *Meurtre pour un homme seul*, 1976)
Khalil Abdul-Muhsen. Director/Regie/réalisation: Richard C. Sarafian.

Robin and Marian (dt. *Robin und Marian*, fr. *La Rose et la Flèche*, 1976)
Robin Hood. Director/Regie/réalisation: Richard Lester.

A Bridge Too Far (dt. *Die Brücke von Arnheim*, fr. *Un pont trop loin*, 1977)
Major General/major général Robert Urquhart. Director/Regie/réalisation: Richard Attenborough.

The First Great Train Robbery (dt. *Der große Eisenbahnraub*, fr. *La Grande Attaque du train d'or*, 1979)
Edward Pierce/John Simms/Geoffrey. Director/Regie/réalisation: Michael Crichton.

Meteor (1979)
Dr. Paul Bradley. Director/Regie/réalisation: Ronald Neame.

Cuba (dt. *Explosion in Kuba*, 1979)
Major Robert Dapes. Director/Regie/réalisation: Richard Lester.

Time Bandits (fr. *Bandits, bandits*, 1981)
King Agamemnon/Fireman//König Agamemnon/Feuerwehrmann//Le roi Agamemnon/un pompier. Director/Regie/réalisation: Terry Gilliam.

Outland (1981)
Marshal William T. O'Niel. Director/Regie/réalisation: Peter Hyams.

Wrong Is Right (dt. *Flammen am Horizont*, fr. *Meurtres en direct*, 1982)
Patrick Hale. Director/Regie/réalisation: Richard Brooks.

Five Days One Summer (dt. *Am Rande des Abgrunds*, fr. *Cinq jours ce printemps-là*, 1982)
Douglas Meredith. Director/Regie/réalisation: Fred Zinnemann.

Never Say Never Again (dt. *Sag niemals nie*, fr. *Jamais plus jamais*, 1983)
James Bond. Director/Regie/réalisation: Irvin Kershner.

Sword of the Valiant: The Legend of Sir Gawain and the Green Knight (dt. *Camelot: Der Fluch des goldenen Schwertes*, fr. *L'Épée du vaillant*, 1984)
The Green Knight/Grüner Ritter/Le Chevalier vert. Director/Regie/réalisation: Stephen Weeks.

Highlander (dt. *Highlander: Es kann nur einen geben*, 1986)
Juan Sanchez Villa-Lobos Ramirez. Director/Regie/réalisation: Russell Mulcahy.

The Name of the Rose (dt. *Der Name der Rose*, fr. *Le Nom de la rose*, 1986)
William of Baskerville/Guillaume de Baskerville. Director/Regie/réalisation: Jean-Jacques Annaud.

The Untouchables (dt. *The Untouchables: Die Unbestechlichen*, fr. *Les Incorruptibles*, 1987)
Jim Malone. Director/Regie/réalisation: Brian De Palma.

The Presidio (dt. *Presidio*, fr. *Presidio, base militaire, San Francisco*, 1988)
Lieutenant Colonel Alan Caldwell. Director/Regie/réalisation: Peter Hyams.

Indiana Jones and the Last Crusade (dt. *Indiana Jones und der letzte Kreuzzug*, fr. *Indiana Jones et la dernière croisade*, 1989)
Professor/Professeur Henry Jones. Director/Regie/réalisation: Steven Spielberg.

Family Business (1989)
Jessie McMullen. Director/Regie/réalisation: Sidney Lumet.

The Hunt for Red October (dt. *Jagd auf Roter Oktober*, fr. *À la poursuite d'Octobre Rouge*, 1990)
Captain/Kapitän/Capitaine Marko Ramius. Director/Regie/réalisation: John McTiernan.

The Russia House (dt. *Das Russland-Haus*, fr. *La Maison Russie*, 1990)
Bartholomew "Barley" Scott Blair. Director/Regie/réalisation: Fred Schepisi.

Highlander II: The Quickening (dt. *Highlander II: Die Rückkehr*, fr. *Highlander, le retour*, 1991)
Juan Sanchez Villa-Lobos Ramirez. Director/Regie/réalisation: Russell Mulcahy.

Robin Hood: Prince of Thieves (dt. *Robin Hood: König der Diebe*, fr. *Robin des Bois, prince des voleurs*, 1991)
King Richard I/König Richard I./le roi Richard. Director/Regie/réalisation: Kevin Reynolds.

Medicine Man (dt. *Medicine Man: Die letzten Tage von Eden*, fr. *Medicine Man, le sorcier de l'océan vert*, 1992)
Dr. Robert Campbell [also executive producer/auch ausführender Produzent/également producteur exécutif]. Director/Regie/réalisation: John McTiernan.

Rising Sun (dt. *Die Wiege der Sonne*, fr. *Soleil levant*, 1993)
Captain John Connor [also executive producer/auch ausführender Produzent/également producteur exécutif]. Director/Regie/réalisation: Philip Kaufman.

A Good Man in Africa (fr. *Un Anglais sous les tropiques*, 1994)
Dr. Alex Murray. Director/Regie/réalisation: Bruce Beresford.

First Knight (dt. *Der 1. Ritter*, fr. *Lancelot*, 1995)
King Arthur/König Arthur/le roi Arthur. Director/Regie/réalisation: Jerry Zucker.

Just Cause (dt. *Im Sumpf des Verbrechens*, fr. *Juste cause*, 1995)
Paul Armstrong [also executive producer/auch ausführender Produzent/également producteur exécutif]. Director/Regie/réalisation: Arne Glimcher.

Dragonheart (fr. *Cœur de dragon*, 1996)
Draco (Voice/Stimme in der Originalfassung/voix originale). Director/Regie/réalisation: Rob Cohen.

The Rock (dt. *The Rock: Fels der Entscheidung*, fr. *Rock*, 1996)
John Patrick Mason [also executive producer/auch ausführender Produzent/également producteur exécutif]. Director/Regie/réalisation: Michael Bay.

The Avengers (dt. *Mit Schirm, Charme und Melone*, fr. *Chapeau melon et bottes de cuir*, 1998)
Sir August de Wynter. Director/Regie/réalisation: Jeremiah S. Chechik

Playing by Heart (dt. *Leben und Lieben in L.A.*, fr. *La Carte du cœur*, 1998)
Paul. Director/Regie/réalisation: Willard Carroll.

Entrapment (dt. *Verlockende Falle*, fr. *Haute voltige*, 1999)
Robert MacDougal [also producer/auch Produzent/également producteur]. Director/Regie/réalisation: Jon Amiel.

Finding Forrester (dt. *Forrester – Gefunden!*, fr. *À la rencontre de Forrester*, 2000)
William Forrester [also producer/auch Produzent/également producteur]. Director/Regie/réalisation: Gus Van Sant.

The League of Extraordinary Gentlemen (dt. *Die Liga der außergewöhnlichen Gentlemen*, fr. *La Ligue des gentlemen extraordinaires*, 2003)
Allan Quatermain [also executive producer/auch ausführender Produzent/également producteur exécutif]. Director/Regie/réalisation: Stephen Norrington.

BIBLIOGRAPHY

Alonso Barahona, Fernando: *Biografía y películas de Sean Connery.* Barcelona, 1992.

Andrews, Emma: *The Films of Sean Connery (Heroes of the Movies).* New York, 1982.

Babington, Bruce: *British Stars and Stardom: From Alma Taylor to Sean Connery.* Manchester, 2002.

Callan, Michael Feeney: *Sean Connery.* London, 2002.

Connery, Sean: *Being a Scot.* London, 2008.

Dupuis, Jean-Jacques: *Sean Connery.* Paris, 1986.

Durant, Philippe: *Sean Connery.* Clamart, 1989.

Freedland, Michael: *Sean Connery: A Biography.* London, 1995.

Gant, Richard: *Sean Connery: Gilt-edged Bond.* London, 1967.

Grassi, Giovanna: *Der Mythos Sean Connery. Ein Star für alle Jahreszeiten.* Marburg, 2001.

Heinzlmeier, Adolf: *Sean Connery. Lizenz zum Filmen.* Hamburg; Vienna, 2001.

Hunter, John: *Great Scot: The Life of Sean Connery.* London, 1994.

Johnstone, Ian: *Sean Connery.* London, 1990.

Lewin, David: *"The Playboy Interview: Sean Connery."* Playboy Magazine, November 1965.

McCabe, Bob: *Sean Connery: A Biography.* New York, 2000.

Moral, Tony Lee: *Hitchcock and the Making of Marnie.* Lanham, 2002.

Norman, Neil: *Sean Connery.* New York, 1984.

Parker, John: *Arise Sir Sean Connery: The Biography of Britain's Greatest Living Actor.* London, 2005.

Passingham, Kenneth: *Sean Connery: A Biography.* New York, 1983.

Pfeiffer, Lee and Philip Lisa: *The Films of Sean Connery.* New York, 2001.

Rissik, Andrew: *The James Bond Man: The Films of Sean Connery.* London, 1983.

Rome International Festival of Cinema: *Sean Connery.* Milan, 2006.

Sellers, Robert: *Sean Connery.* London, 2000.

Simpson, Rachel: *The Unofficial Sean Connery.* Bath, 1996.

Tanitch, Robert: *Sean Connery.* London, 1992.

Tesche, Siegfried: *Sean Connery: Sein Leben, Seine Filme.* Berlin, 2005.

Turner, Adrian: *Goldfinger: The Ultimate A-Z.* London, 1998.

Winder, Simon: *The Man Who Saved Britain: A Personal Journey into the Disturbing World of James Bond.* New York, 2007.

Yule, Andrew: *Sean Connery: Neither Shaken Nor Stirred.* London, 1993.

IMPRINT

© 2009 TASCHEN GmbH
Hohenzollernring 53, D-50672 Köln
www.taschen.com

Editor/Picture Research: Paul Duncan/Wordsmith Solutions
Editorial Coordination: Martin Holz, Cologne
Production Coordination: Nadia Najm, Cologne
German Translation: Thomas J. Kinne, Nauheim
French Translation: Alice Pétillot, Paris
Multilingual Production: www.arnaudbriand.com, Paris
Typeface Design: Sense/Net, Andy Disl and Birgi Eichwede, Cologne

Printed in China
ISBN 978-3-8365-0857-5

To stay informed about upcoming TASCHEN titles, please request our magazine at www.taschen.com/magazine or write to TASCHEN, Hohenzollernring 53, D-50672 Cologne, Germany, contact@taschen.com, Fax: +49-221-254919. We will be happy to send you a free copy of our magazine which is filled with information about all of our books.

7/132

WITHDRAWN